MW01641323

Income Tax Made Easy

A Beginner's Guide

Second Edition

PATRICIA PETHERBRIDGE-HERNANDEZ
AND
KATHLEEN P. O'DONNELL

1 2 3 4 5 6 7 8 9 10
ISBN 0-8251-3870-1
Copyright © 1994, 1999
J. Weston Walch, Publisher
P. O. Box 658 • Portland, Maine 04104-0658
Printed in the United States of America

We wish to acknowledge

the invaluable contributions of

Stephen O'Donnell, CPA, to this book.

Contents

CHAPTER 1

Introduction

If you earn money, you probably have to pay taxes on what you earn (your income). To figure out how much you must pay in taxes, you must fill out an income tax return every year. Filling out the form may not be easy, and parting with your hard-earned money may be painful. But doing this is your duty as a worker in the United States. It's part of being a member of our society. It's also the law.

Like many people, you may think it's too difficult and confusing to do your own tax return. That's not necessarily so. This course will take you step by step through the process, one form and one step at a time. You'll learn how to take care of this civic responsibility on your own.

This chapter introduces you to the course. In this chapter, we discuss the following items:

- Objectives
- Concepts
- Activities
- Benefits
- Disclaimer

OBJECTIVES

You will learn to:

- Explain what the federal income tax is.
- Explain your filing responsibilities and deadlines.
- Fill out the simple forms most people use.
- Obtain more information about federal income taxes.

CONCEPTS

The concepts we will discuss include:

- What is the income tax?
- Withholding
- Filing a tax return: concepts and deadlines
- Filing procedures

- Types of forms
- Filling out forms—1040EZ and 1040A
- Where you can get help

ACTIVITIES

Activities include:

- Exercises with tax-related concepts.
- Exercises to help you practice using tax-related vocabulary.
- Exercises to help you understand how the concepts relate to your situation.
- Practice in filling out sample forms.

BENEFITS

Why is this information important to you?

- You will have a better understanding of the process of paying taxes.
- Almost everyone who works must pay taxes and send in a tax return form.
- This is your civic responsibility, and it is the law.
- You may need your tax return forms for immigration matters.
- You may get money back when you send in your tax return form.
- You may be able to fill out the forms by yourself without paying someone else to do it.
- If you need help filling out the form, you will learn ways to get that help for free.

DISCLAIMER

This book is intended to be an introduction to the basic concepts of income taxes and filing income tax returns.

It is not intended to be used as professional tax advice.

If you need more information, you should contact the Internal Revenue Service (IRS), an accountant, or a professional tax preparer.

Rules and information change from year to year. Be sure to check the information and instructions for the current year.

CHAPTER 2

What Is Income Tax?

In this chapter, you will learn about:

- What kinds of income taxes there are.
- What federal income tax is used for.
- How much the government spends.
- Where the money goes.
- How the money is distributed.
- Benefits you receive.
- What kind of income is taxed.
- What kind of income is not taxed.

VOCABULARY

ACTIVITY: The definition for each of these words is in the Glossary. As a vocabulary exercise, you may try to write a definition for each word before you look up its meaning in the Glossary.

federal

state

income

tax

IRS (Internal Revenue Service)

earnings

WHAT KINDS OF TAXES ARE THERE?

You must pay more than one kind of tax on what you earn.

- **Federal income tax**

  You pay a tax on your income to the United States (federal) government.

  The IRS is the government agency that is responsible for collecting income tax.

- **Social Security tax**

  You pay this tax to the federal government. Retired people and disabled people often receive Social Security payments.

- **Medicare**

  You pay this tax to the federal government. It provides medical insurance for senior citizens.

  Social Security tax and Medicare tax used to be combined and were called FICA (Federal Insurance Contributions Act).

- **State income tax**

  Most states require you to pay an income tax to the state. This is in addition to federal income tax.

- **Other**

  Many states have some other form of tax. For example, California has a tax called SDI (State Disability Insurance).

WHAT IS FEDERAL INCOME TAX USED FOR?

Your federal income taxes are used for many programs, for example:

1. National defense
2. Transportation
3. Health
4. Agriculture
5. Education
6. International affairs
7. Science, energy, research

HOW MUCH DOES THE GOVERNMENT SPEND?

In the year 1997, the federal government:

- Received $1,579,000,000,000
- Spent $1,601,000,000,000

There was a deficit of $22,000,000,000.

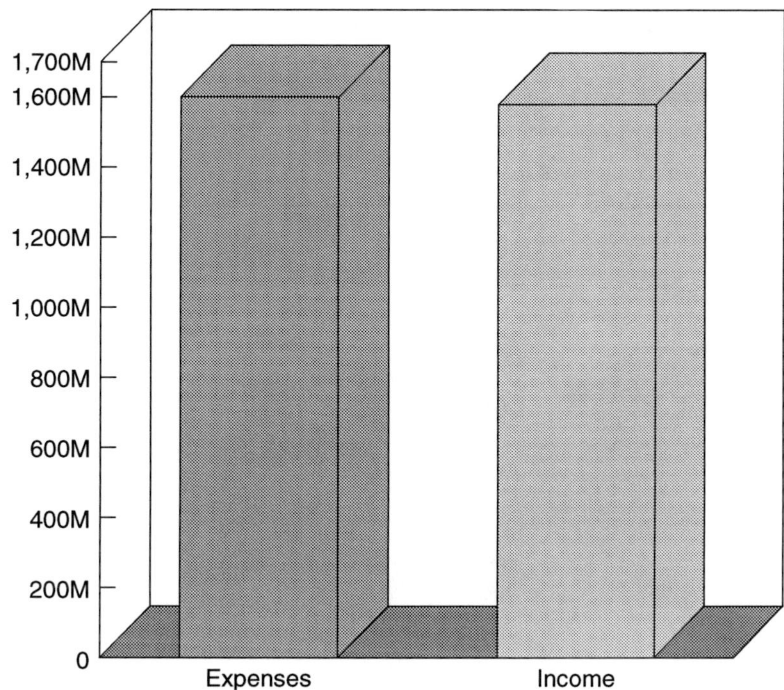

These figures are provided by the federal government. In the chart, the *M* stands for "million." 200M is equal to 200,000,000, or 200 million.

WHERE DOES THE MONEY GO?

Here's how the federal government spent the money:

• Social Security and Medicare	$ 608,380,000,000	38%
• National defense	$ 320,200,000,000	20%
• Interest payments	$ 240,150,000,000	15%
• Social programs	$ 192,120,000,000	12%
• Human and community development	$ 112,070,000,000	7%
• Health	$ 96,060,000,000	6%
• Law enforcement	$ 32,020,000,000	2%
Total	$1,601,000,000,000	100%

HOW IS THE MONEY DISTRIBUTED?

Activity: The following chart shows the proportion of how the federal income taxes are distributed. Write in the percentage for each category.

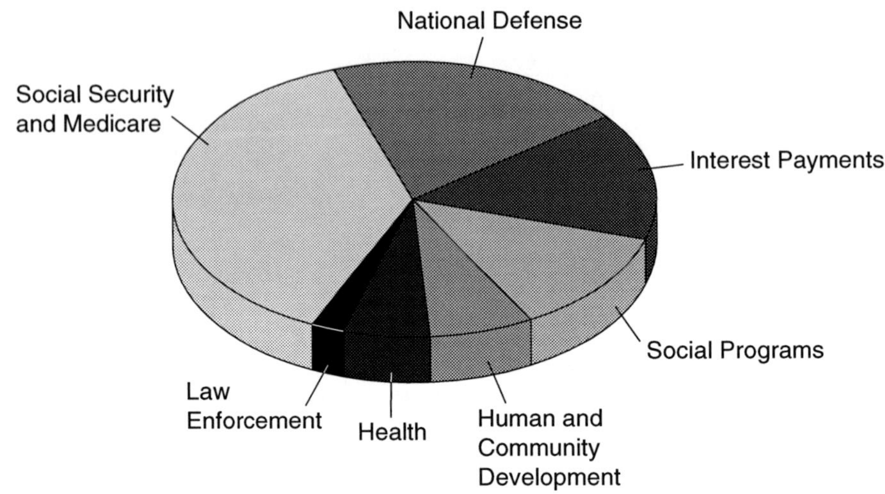

DO YOU RECEIVE BENEFITS?

Activity: Check ☑ each of the programs that you benefit from.

Do you benefit from federal government programs? Here are some common programs:

- ☐ Social Security
- ☐ Grants to schools
- ☐ Medical research
- ☐ Highways
- ☐ Air traffic control
- ☐ Veterans' benefits
- ☐ Medicare

WHAT KIND OF INCOME IS TAXED?

Income is earnings, or money, you receive.

- It is important to understand what income can be taxed.
- Most, but not all income is taxed.

Examples of income that can be taxed:

- ☐ Wages and salaries
- ☐ Tips
- ☐ Interest and dividends
- ☐ Rental income
- ☐ Gambling and lottery winnings
- ☐ Income from your own business

ACTIVITY: Check ☑ each of the programs that you benefit from.

WHAT KIND OF INCOME IS NOT TAXED?

Some money you receive is not taxed. Examples of income that is usually not taxed include:

- ☐ Accident and health insurance benefits
- ☐ Welfare benefits
- ☐ Workers' compensation benefits

ACTIVITY: Check ☑ each kind of nontaxable income that you receive.

CHAPTER 3

What Is Withholding?

In this chapter, you will learn about:

- Withholding
- Tax returns
- W-4 forms

VOCABULARY

ACTIVITY: The definition for each of these words is in the Glossary. As a vocabulary exercise, you may try to write a definition for each word before you look up its meaning in the Glossary.

employer

withhold

gross pay

net pay

tax return

W-4 form

WITHHOLDING

If you are employed, the law requires your employer to withhold a part of your income to pay your taxes.

- The employer sends this money to the federal government.
- The amount of money the employer withholds during the year is an estimate of your total tax bill.

TAX RETURN

Since everybody's situation is different, too much or too little money may be withheld from your salary to pay your tax bill.

- The tax return is used to calculate your exact tax bill.
- If too much tax is withheld, you receive a refund when you file your tax return form.
- If not enough tax is withheld, you must pay more when you file your tax return form.

W-4 FORM

You tell the employer how much to withhold by filling out a W-4 form. You can fill out a new W-4 form at any time. Usually, you fill out a W-4 form in the following situations:

- You start a new job.
- You get married or divorced.
- You have a child.
- Your child moves out and no longer receives your financial support.

This form tells your employer how much tax to withhold from your salary. You need a W-4 form for each employer. If you have two jobs, you must fill out a W-4 form for each employer.

W-4 FORM—PAGE 1

Form W-4 (1999)

Purpose. Complete Form W-4 so your employer can withhold the correct Federal income tax from your pay. Because your tax situation may change, you may want to refigure your withholding each year.

Exemption from withholding. If you are exempt, complete only lines 1, 2, 3, 4, and 7, and sign the form to validate it. Your exemption for 1999 expires February 16, 2000.

Note: *You cannot claim exemption from withholding if (1) your income exceeds $700 and includes more than $250 of unearned income (e.g., interest and dividends) and (2) another person can claim you as a dependent on their tax return.*

Basic instructions. If you are not exempt, complete the Personal Allowances Worksheet. The worksheets on page 2 adjust your withholding allowances based on itemized deductions, adjustments to income, or two-earner/two-job situations. Complete all worksheets that apply. They will help you figure the number of withholding allowances you are entitled to claim. **However, you may claim fewer allowances.**

Child tax and higher education credits. For details on adjusting withholding for these and other credits, see **Pub. 919,** Is My Withholding Correct for 1999?

Head of household. Generally, you may claim head of household filing status on your tax return only if you are unmarried and pay more than 50% of the costs of keeping up a home for yourself and your dependent(s) or other qualifying individuals. See line **E** below.

Nonwage income. If you have a large amount of nonwage income, such as interest or dividends, you should consider making estimated tax payments using Form 1040-ES. Otherwise, you may owe additional tax.

Two earners/two jobs. If you have a working spouse or more than one job, figure the total number of allowances you are entitled to claim on all jobs using worksheets from only one Form W-4. Your withholding will usually be most accurate when all allowances are claimed on the Form W-4 prepared for the highest paying job and zero allowances are claimed for the others.

Check your withholding. After your Form W-4 takes effect, use Pub. 919 to see how the dollar amount you are having withheld compares to your estimated total annual tax. Get Pub. 919 especially if you used the Two-Earner/Two-Job Worksheet and your earnings exceed $150,000 (Single) or $200,000 (Married).

Recent name change? If your name on line 1 differs from that shown on your social security card, call 1-800-772-1213 for a new social security card.

Personal Allowances Worksheet

A Enter "1" for **yourself** if no one else can claim you as a dependent . . . . **A** ______

B Enter "1" if:
- You are single and have only one job; or
- You are married, have only one job, and your spouse does not work; or
- Your wages from a second job or your spouse's wages (the total of both) are $1,000 or less.

. . **B** ______

C Enter "1" for your **spouse.** But, you may choose to enter -0- if you are married and have either a working spouse or more than one job. (This may help you avoid having too little tax withheld.) . . . . **C** ______

D Enter number of **dependents** (other than your spouse or yourself) you will claim on your tax return . . . . . . **D** ______

E Enter "1" if you will file as **head of household** on your tax return (see conditions under **Head of household** above) . **E** ______

F Enter "1" if you have at least $1,500 of **child or dependent care expenses** for which you plan to claim a credit . . **F** ______

G **Child Tax Credit:** • If your total income will be between $20,000 and $50,000 ($23,000 and $63,000 if married), enter "1" for each eligible child. • If your total income will be between $50,000 and $80,000 ($63,000 and $115,000 if married), enter "1" if you have two eligible children, enter "2" if you have three or four eligible children, or enter "3" if you have five or more eligible children . . **G** ______

H Add lines A through G and enter total here. **Note:** This amount may be different from the number of exemptions you claim on your return. ▶ **H** ______

For accuracy, complete all worksheets that apply.
- If you plan to **itemize or claim adjustments to income** and want to reduce your withholding, see the Deductions and Adjustments Worksheet on page 2.
- If you are **single,** have **more than one job** and your combined earnings from all jobs exceed $32,000, OR if you are **married** and have a **working spouse or more than one job** and the combined earnings from all jobs exceed $55,000, see the Two-Earner/Two-Job Worksheet on page 2 to avoid having too little tax withheld.
- If **neither** of the above situations applies, **stop here** and enter the number from line H on line 5 of Form W-4 below.

Cut here and give the certificate to your employer. Keep the top part for your records.

Form **W-4**
Department of the Treasury
Internal Revenue Service

Employee's Withholding Allowance Certificate

▶ **For Privacy Act and Paperwork Reduction Act Notice, see page 2.**

OMB No. 1545-0010

1999

1 Type or print your first name and middle initial | Last name | 2 Your social security number

Home address (number and street or rural route)

3 ☐ Single ☐ Married ☐ Married, but withhold at higher Single rate.
Note: *If married, but legally separated, or spouse is a nonresident alien, check the Single box.*

City or town, state, and ZIP code

4 If your last name differs from that on your social security card, check here. **You** must call 1-800-772-1213 for a new card . . . ▶ ☐

5 Total number of allowances you are claiming (from line H above or from the worksheets on page 2 if they apply) | 5 |

6 Additional amount, if any, you want withheld from each paycheck . . . . | 6 | $

7 I claim exemption from withholding for 1999, and I certify that I meet **BOTH** of the following conditions for exemption:
- Last year I had a right to a refund of **ALL** Federal income tax withheld because I had **NO** tax liability **AND**
- This year I expect a refund of **ALL** Federal income tax withheld because I expect to have **NO** tax liability.

If you meet both conditions, write "EXEMPT" here . . . . ▶ | 7 |

Under penalties of perjury, I certify that I am entitled to the number of withholding allowances claimed on this certificate, or I am entitled to claim exempt status.

Employee's signature
(Form is not valid unless you sign it) ▶ **Date** ▶

8 Employer's name and address (Employer: Complete 8 and 10 only if sending to the IRS) | 9 Office code (optional) | 10 Employer identification number

Cat. No. 10220Q

W-4 FORM—PAGE 2

Form W-4 (1999) Page **2**

Deductions and Adjustments Worksheet

Note: *Use this worksheet only if you plan to itemize deductions or claim adjustments to income on your 1999 tax return.*

1	Enter an estimate of your 1999 itemized deductions. These include qualifying home mortgage interest, charitable contributions, state and local taxes (but not sales taxes), medical expenses in excess of 7.5% of your income, and miscellaneous deductions. (For 1999, you may have to reduce your itemized deductions if your income is over $126,600 ($63,300 if married filing separately). Get Pub. 919 for details.)	**1**	$
2	Enter: { $7,200 if married filing jointly or qualifying widow(er); $6,350 if head of household; $4,300 if single; $3,600 if married filing separately }	**2**	$
3	**Subtract** line 2 from line 1. If line 2 is greater than line 1, enter -0-	**3**	$
4	Enter an estimate of your 1999 adjustments to income, including alimony, deductible IRA contributions, and student loan interest .	**4**	$
5	**Add** lines 3 and 4 and enter the total	**5**	$
6	Enter an estimate of your 1999 nonwage income (such as dividends or interest)	**6**	$
7	**Subtract** line 6 from line 5. Enter the result, but not less than -0-	**7**	$
8	**Divide** the amount on line 7 by $3,000 and enter the result here. Drop any fraction	**8**	
9	Enter the number from Personal Allowances Worksheet, line H, on page 1	**9**	
10	**Add** lines 8 and 9 and enter the total here. If you plan to use the Two-Earner/Two-Job Worksheet, also enter this total on line 1 below. Otherwise, **stop here** and enter this total on Form W-4, line 5, on page 1 . . .	**10**	

Two-Earner/Two-Job Worksheet

Note: *Use this worksheet only if the instructions for line H on page 1 direct you here.*

1	Enter the number from line H on page 1 (or from line 10 above if you used the Deductions and Adjustments Worksheet)			**1**	
2	Find the number in **Table 1** below that applies to the **LOWEST** paying job and enter it here . . .			**2**	
3	If line 1 is **GREATER THAN OR EQUAL TO** line 2, subtract line 2 from line 1. Enter the result here (if zero, enter -0-) and on Form W-4, line 5, on page 1. **DO NOT** use the rest of this worksheet . . .			**3**	
Note:	*If line 1 is **LESS THAN** line 2, enter -0- on Form W-4, line 5, on page 1. Complete lines 4–9 to calculate the additional withholding amount necessary to avoid a year end tax bill.*				
4	Enter the number from line 2 of this worksheet	**4**			
5	Enter the number from line 1 of this worksheet	**5**			
6	**Subtract** line 5 from line 4			**6**	
7	Find the amount in **Table 2** below that applies to the **HIGHEST** paying job and enter it here . . .			**7**	$
8	**Multiply** line 7 by line 6 and enter the result here. This is the additional annual withholding amount needed			**8**	$
9	Divide line 8 by the number of pay periods remaining in 1999. (For example, divide by 26 if you are paid every other week and you complete this form in December 1998.) Enter the result here and on Form W-4, line 6, page 1. This is the additional amount to be withheld from each paycheck			**9**	$

Table 1: Two-Earner/Two-Job Worksheet

Married Filing Jointly				All Others			
If wages from **LOWEST** paying job are—	Enter on line 2 above	If wages from **LOWEST** paying job are—	Enter on line 2 above	If wages from **LOWEST** paying job are—	Enter on line 2 above	If wages from **LOWEST** paying job are—	Enter on line 2 above
$0 - $4,000	0	40,001 - 45,000	8	$0 - $5,000	0	65,001 - 80,000	8
4,001 - 7,000	1	45,001 - 54,000	9	5,001 - 11,000	1	80,001 - 100,000	9
7,001 - 12,000	2	54,001 - 62,000	10	11,001 - 16,000	2	100,001 and over	10
12,001 - 18,000	3	62,001 - 70,000	11	16,001 - 21,000	3		
18,001 - 24,000	4	70,001 - 85,000	12	21,001 - 25,000	4		
24,001 - 28,000	5	85,001 - 100,000	13	25,001 - 40,000	5		
28,001 - 35,000	6	100,001 - 110,000	14	40,001 - 50,000	6		
35,001 - 40,000	7	110,001 and over	15	50,001 - 65,000	7		

Table 2: Two-Earner/Two-Job Worksheet

Married Filing Jointly		All Others	
If wages from **HIGHEST** paying job are—	Enter on line 7 above	If wages from **HIGHEST** paying job are—	Enter on line 7 above
$0 - $50,000	$400	$0 - $30,000	$400
50,001 - 100,000	770	30,001 - 60,000	770
100,001 - 130,000	850	60,001 - 120,000	850
130,001 - 240,000	1,000	120,001 - 250,000	1,000
240,001 and over	1,100	250,001 and over	1,100

Privacy Act and Paperwork Reduction Act Notice. We ask for the information on this form to carry out the Internal Revenue laws of the United States. The Internal Revenue Code requires this information under sections 3402(f)(2)(A) and 6109 and their regulations. Failure to provide a **properly** completed form will result in your being treated as a single person who claims no withholding allowances; **providing fraudulent information may also subject you to penalties.** Routine uses of this information include giving it to the Department of Justice for civil and criminal litigation and to cities, states, and the District of Columbia for use in administering their tax laws.

You are not required to provide the information requested on a form that is subject to the Paperwork Reduction Act unless the form displays a valid OMB control number. Books or records relating to a form or its instructions must be retained as long as their contents may become material in the administration of any Internal Revenue law. Generally, tax returns and return information are confidential, as required by Code section 6103.

The time needed to complete this form will vary depending on individual circumstances. The estimated average time is: **Recordkeeping** 46 min., **Learning about the law or the form** 10 min., **Preparing the form** 1 hr., 10 min. If you have comments concerning the accuracy of these time estimates or suggestions for making this form simpler, we would be happy to hear from you. You can write to the Tax Forms Committee, Western Area Distribution Center, Rancho Cordova, CA 95743-0001. **DO NOT** send the tax form to this address. Instead, give it to your employer.

W-4 FORM—ACTIVITY 1

ACTIVITY: Complete the W-4 form for the taxpayer described below. Use the instructions and worksheets on the blank form on the previous two pages. You do not need to complete sections 8, 9, and 10.

Joe Hernandez is single and has no dependents. He does not want any additional amount withheld. He lives at 300 Primavera Street, Apt. A, Impuesto, CA 90000. His Social Security number: 123-45-6789.

Cut here and give the certificate to your employer. Keep the top part for your records.

Form **W-4**
Department of the Treasury
Internal Revenue Service

Employee's Withholding Allowance Certificate

► **For Privacy Act and Paperwork Reduction Act Notice, see page 2.**

OMB No. 1545-0010

1999

1 Type or print your first name and middle initial | Last name | **2** Your social security number

Home address (number and street or rural route)

3 ☐ Single ☐ Married ☐ Married, but withhold at higher Single rate.
Note: *If married, but legally separated, or spouse is a nonresident alien, check the Single box.*

City or town, state, and ZIP code

4 If your last name differs from that on your social security card, check here. **You** must call 1-800-772-1213 for a new card . . . ► ☐

5 Total number of allowances you are claiming (from line H above or from the worksheets on page 2 if they apply) . **5**

6 Additional amount, if any, you want withheld from each paycheck . . . . **6** $

7 I claim exemption from withholding for 1999, and I certify that I meet **BOTH** of the following conditions for exemption:
- Last year I had a right to a refund of **ALL** Federal income tax withheld because I had **NO** tax liability **AND**
- This year I expect a refund of **ALL** Federal income tax withheld because I expect to have **NO** tax liability.

If you meet both conditions, write "EXEMPT" here . . . . ► **7**

Under penalties of perjury, I certify that I am entitled to the number of withholding allowances claimed on this certificate, or I am entitled to claim exempt status.
Employee's signature
(Form is not valid unless you sign it) ► **Date** ►

8 Employer's name and address (Employer: Complete 8 and 10 only if sending to the IRS) | **9** Office code (optional) | **10** Employer identification number

Cat. No. 10220Q

W-4 FORM—ACTIVITY 2

ACTIVITY: Complete the W-4 form for the following taxpayer. Use the instructions and worksheets on the blank form on the previous pages. You do not need to complete sections 8, 9, and 10.

Joyce Johnson is married and has two children. She and her husband will claim a total of four exemptions. She will claim two on her W-4 form, and her husband will claim two on his. She does not want any additional amount withheld. She lives at 4300 Lakeview Avenue, Midville, TX 70000. Her Social Security number is 987-65-4321.

Cut here and give the certificate to your employer. Keep the top part for your records.

Form **W-4**
Department of the Treasury
Internal Revenue Service

Employee's Withholding Allowance Certificate

▶ **For Privacy Act and Paperwork Reduction Act Notice, see page 2.**

OMB No. 1545-0010

1999

1 Type or print your first name and middle initial | Last name | 2 Your social security number

Home address (number and street or rural route)

3 ☐ Single ☐ Married ☐ Married, but withhold at higher Single rate.
Note: *If married, but legally separated, or spouse is a nonresident alien, check the Single box.*

City or town, state, and ZIP code

4 If your last name differs from that on your social security card, check here. **You** must call 1-800-772-1213 for a new card . . . ▶ ☐

5 Total number of allowances you are claiming (from line H above or from the worksheets on page 2 if they apply) . | 5 |

6 Additional amount, if any, you want withheld from each paycheck . . . . | 6 | $

7 I claim exemption from withholding for 1999, and I certify that I meet **BOTH** of the following conditions for exemption:
- Last year I had a right to a refund of **ALL** Federal income tax withheld because I had **NO** tax liability **AND**
- This year I expect a refund of **ALL** Federal income tax withheld because I expect to have **NO** tax liability.

If you meet both conditions, write "EXEMPT" here . . . . ▶ | 7 |

Under penalties of perjury, I certify that I am entitled to the number of withholding allowances claimed on this certificate, or I am entitled to claim exempt status.
Employee's signature
(Form is not valid
unless you sign it) ▶ **Date** ▶

8 Employer's name and address (Employer: Complete 8 and 10 only if sending to the IRS) | 9 Office code (optional) | 10 Employer identification number

Cat. No. 10220Q

SAMPLE PAY STUBS

Pay stub A

Name	Social Security No.	Pay Period	Pay Date
Hernandez, Joe	123-45-6789	Ends 12/24/98	12/31/98
Hours/Units	Rate	Earnings	Deductions
80.00	8.93	714.40	0.00

	Gross Pay	Federal Income Tax	Soc. Sec. Tax	Medicare Tax	State Tax	SDI	Net pay
This pay	714.40	78.00	44.29	10.36	12.37	9.29	560.09
YTD	15,000.00	1,638.00	930.00	217.50	259.77	195.09	11,759.64

Pay stub B

Name	Social Security No.	Pay Period	Pay Date
Johnson, Joyce	987-65-4321	Ends 12/24/98	12/31/98
Hours/Units	**Rate**	**Earnings**	**Deductions**
48	6.09	292.32	0.00

	Gross Pay	Federal Income Tax	Soc. Sec. Tax	Medicare Tax	State Tax	City Tax	Net pay
This pay	292.32	8.00	18.12	4.24	2.00	3.80	256.16
YTD	7,600.00	208.00	471.10	110.20	52.00	48.80	6,709.90

WITHHOLDING ACTIVITY

ACTIVITY: Look at the sample pay stubs. If you have a copy of your own pay stub, use it also. For each stub, fill in the following items for the current pay period.

Item	Pay Stub A	Pay Stub B	Your Pay Stub
Salary (or gross pay)			
Federal income tax withheld			
State income tax withheld			
Social Security tax withheld			
Medicare tax withheld			
Other withheld			
Net pay (take-home pay)			

CHAPTER 4

Filing Concepts and Deadlines

In this chapter, you will learn about:

- Your filing status
- Who must file
- Dependents
- Filing if not required
- What happens when you file
- What happens if you make a mistake
- Penalties
- Deadlines
- Social Security numbers
- Individual Taxpayer Identification Numbers (ITINs)

VOCABULARY

ACTIVITY: The definition for each of these words is in the Glossary. As a vocabulary exercise, you may try to write a definition for each word before you look up its meaning in the Glossary.

filing status

head of household

support

widow/widower

dependent

earned income credit

penalty

audit

deadline

WHAT IS YOUR FILING STATUS?

Your filing status is how you define your family situation for tax purposes.

☐ **Single person**

A single individual or a divorced individual.

☐ **Head of household**

An unmarried person who shared and maintained a home for himself/herself and a qualifying relative for more than six months. Examples of qualifying relatives are children, in-laws, grandparents, grandchildren, brother, and sister.

An unmarried person who maintained the main home for a parent for the whole year. The parent and unmarried person may live in separate homes.

A married person who is separated AND supported himself/herself and a son or a daughter in a shared home for more than six months AND lived apart from the spouse during the last six months of the filing year AND who files a separate tax return.

☐ **Widow or widower with dependent child**

A widow or widower who has not remarried AND whose spouse died during the previous two years AND who has at least one dependent child.

☐ **Married couple, filing together (jointly)**

A married couple.

A person who became a widow or widower during the filing year.

☐ **Married couple, filing separately**

A married couple who file separate returns. Each spouse filing separately is charged at a higher rate than if the couple filed together.

WHO MUST FILE?

ACTIVITY: Place a check next to the category that applies to you. If no category applies, you probably are not required to file.

For the 1998 tax year, you had to file if you were in one of the following groups:

Age	Who earned more than
☐ Single persons	
Under 65	$6,950.00
65 or over	$8,000.00

☐ Married persons, filing together (jointly)	
Both under 65	$12,500.00
One under 65, one 65 or over	$13,350.00
Both 65 or over	$14,200.00
☐ Married persons, filing separately	
Any age	$2,700.00
☐ Widows or widowers with dependent child	
Under 65	$9,800.00
65 or over	$10,650.00

WHO IS A DEPENDENT?

People who are supported by others are generally considered dependents. If you have children or other close relatives whom you support, you can claim them as dependents on your form. You receive a deduction on your taxes for each dependent.

Five requirements must be met to qualify as a dependent.

☐ **The person filing the tax form must provide more than half of the support of the dependent.**

Support includes rent, food, clothes, medical expenses, educational expenses, and so on.

☐ **The dependent cannot earn more than $2,700.00.**

This does not apply to your child under age 19 or your child who is a full-time student under age 24.

☐ **The dependent must live for the entire year with the person filing the income tax return *unless* she or he is a relative.**

Son, daughter, grandchild, parent, grandparent, brother, sister, brother-in-law, sister-in-law, mother-in-law, father-in-law, and if related by blood, uncle, aunt, niece, or nephew.

If the dependent is a cousin, he or she must live in the taxpayer's home.

☐ **The dependent must be a resident of the United States, Canada, or Mexico.**

☐ **If the dependent is married, he or she must not file a joint income tax return with his or her spouse.**

WHO ARE YOUR DEPENDENTS?

ACTIVITY: List all your dependents here. Make certain that they meet all five requirements listed previously.

1. ______________________
2. ______________________
3. ______________________
4. ______________________
5. ______________________
6. ______________________

SHOULD YOU FILE IF NOT REQUIRED?

Sometimes it is a good idea to file a tax return even if you are not required to do so. You should file if:

- **You had income tax withheld from your pay.**

  You may get a refund.

- **You qualify for the earned income credit.**

  This is a refundable credit of up to $3,756.00.

- **Your income must be less than $30,095.00.**

  If the credit is larger than your tax, the difference will be refunded to you.

WHAT HAPPENS WHEN YOU FILE?

Usually, when you file, one of two things will happen:

- **You will get money back.**

  The refund check will come in the mail, or you can choose to have your refund deposited directly into your bank account.

  If you do not get your refund within eight weeks, call the IRS.

OR

- **You will owe more money to pay your taxes.**

  Pay the amount you owe when you send in your tax return form.

  If you cannot pay the whole amount, send in the tax return form on time with a partial payment. The IRS will bill you for the balance, plus interest.

If you get a lot of money back, or if you owe a lot of money, you should think about changing the amount of money withheld from what you earn.

- **To do this, submit a new W-4 form to your employer.**

  The W-4 form is described in Chapter 3.

WHAT IF YOU MAKE A MISTAKE?

Amended returns

- If after you file you find out you made a mistake, you may file an amended return.

Audits

- The IRS may audit your tax return. This means that the IRS reviews your income tax return. If the IRS finds a mistake, you may have to pay more taxes, plus interest. Sometimes there is also a penalty.

PENALTIES FOR NOT FILING OR FOR MISTAKES

Civil penalties

You may have to pay penalties if you:

- Are required to file a return and don't file.
- File late.
- Don't pay enough taxes.
- Make serious mistakes.
- Commit fraud.

These penalties are extra payments, in addition to taxes and interest.

Criminal penalties

If you commit serious fraud, you may be brought to trial. In addition to making penalty payments, you could be sent to jail.

DEADLINES

The deadlines for filing your income tax return form is:

- **April 15.**

  Or the following Monday if April 15 falls on a weekend.

- **Your form must be postmarked no later than April 15.**

  Some post offices stay open late on April 15.

- **Don't wait until the last minute!**

Extensions

You can get an extension if you need one.

- An automatic four-month extension is granted if you complete and send Form 4868 by April 15.
- If you owe money, you must still pay the amount you owe by April 15.
- If you are going to receive a refund, you will get it later if you use an extension.
- Usually, extensions are used by people with complicated tax situations.

SOCIAL SECURITY NUMBERS

000-00-0000

Who needs one?

- Anyone who files a tax return form.
- Dependents (for example, your children).

Where do you get it?

- File a Form SS-5 with your local Social Security Administration office.
- Call the office to find out what documentation you need to prove your age, identity, and citizenship.

FORM SS-5

Form Approved
OMB No. 0960-0066

SOCIAL SECURITY ADMINISTRATION Application for a Social Security Card

1	**NAME** TO BE SHOWN ON CARD →	First / Full Middle Name / Last
	FULL NAME AT BIRTH IF OTHER THAN ABOVE →	First / Full Middle Name / Last
	OTHER NAMES USED →	
2	**MAILING ADDRESS** Do Not Abbreviate →	Street Address, Apt. No., PO Box, Rural Route No. City / State / Zip Code
3	**CITIZENSHIP** (Check One) →	☐ U.S. Citizen ☐ Legal Alien Allowed To Work ☐ Legal Alien **Not** Allowed To Work ☐ Other (See Instructions On Page 1)
4	**SEX** →	☐ Male ☐ Female
5	**RACE/ETHNIC DESCRIPTION** (Check One Only–Voluntary) →	☐ Asian, Asian-American or Pacific Islander ☐ Hispanic ☐ Black (Not Hispanic) ☐ North American Indian or Alaskan Native ☐ White (Not Hispanic)
6	**DATE OF BIRTH** ______ Month, Day, Year	**7** **PLACE OF BIRTH** (Do Not Abbreviate) City / State or Foreign Country / FCI — Office Use Only
8	**A. MOTHER'S MAIDEN NAME** →	First / Full Middle Name / Last Name At Her Birth
	B. MOTHER'S SOCIAL SECURITY NUMBER (Complete only if applying for a number for a child under age 18.) →	☐☐☐-☐☐-☐☐☐☐
9	**A. FATHER'S NAME** →	First / Full Middle Name / Last
	B. FATHER'S SOCIAL SECURITY NUMBER (Complete only if applying for a number for a child under age 18.) →	☐☐☐-☐☐-☐☐☐☐
10	Has the applicant or anyone acting on his/her behalf ever filed for or received a Social Security number card before?	☐ Yes (If "yes," answer questions 11-13.) ☐ No (If "no," go on to question 14.) ☐ Don't Know (If "don't know," go on to question 14.)
11	Enter the Social Security number previously assigned to the person listed in item 1. →	☐☐☐-☐☐-☐☐☐☐
12	Enter the name shown on the most recent Social Security card issued for the person listed in item 1. →	First / Middle / Last
13	Enter any different date of birth if used on an earlier application for a card. →	______ Month, Day, Year
14	**TODAY'S DATE** ______ Month, Day, Year	**15** **DAYTIME PHONE NUMBER** ( ) Area Code / Number

DELIBERATELY FURNISHING (OR CAUSING TO BE FURNISHED) FALSE INFORMATION ON THIS APPLICATION IS A CRIME PUNISHABLE BY FINE OR IMPRISONMENT, OR BOTH.

16	**YOUR SIGNATURE** ▶ ______	**17** **YOUR RELATIONSHIP TO THE PERSON IN ITEM 1 IS:** ☐ Self ☐ Natural or Adoptive Parent ☐ Legal Guardian ☐ Other (Specify) ______

INDIVIDUAL TAXPAYER IDENTIFICATION NUMBERS (ITINs)

000-00-0000

Who needs one?

- Any taxpayer or dependent who is not eligible for a Social Security number.

Where do you get it?

- File a Form W-7 with your local Internal Revenue Service office.
- Call the office to find out what documentation you need to submit with the W-7.

Form **W-7** (Rev. February 1998)
Department of the Treasury Internal Revenue Service

Application for IRS Individual Taxpayer Identification Number

▶ See instructions. ▶ Please type or print.
▶ For use by individuals who are NOT U.S. citizens, nationals, or permanent residents.

OMB No. 1545-1483

Please note the following when completing this form:

- *This number is for tax purposes only.* ***Do not submit*** *this form if you have, or are eligible to obtain, a U.S. social security number (SSN).*
- *Receipt of an ITIN creates no inference regarding your immigration status or your right to work in the United States.*
- *Receipt of an ITIN does not make you eligible to claim the earned income credit (EIC).*

FOR IRS USE ONLY

Reason you are submitting Form W-7. (Check only one box. See instructions.)

a ☐ Nonresident alien required to obtain ITIN to claim tax treaty benefit
b ☐ Nonresident alien filing a U.S. tax return and not eligible for an SSN
c ☐ U.S. resident alien (based on days present in the United States) filing a U.S. tax return and not eligible for an SSN
d ☐ Dependent of U.S. person } Enter name and SSN of U.S. person (see instructions) ▶
e ☐ Spouse of U.S. person
f ☐ Other (specify)

1 Name (see instructions)	1a Last name (surname or family name)	First name	Middle name
Name at birth if different . . ▶	1b Last name (surname or family name)	First name	Middle name
2 Permanent residence address, if any (see instructions)	Street address, apartment number, or rural route number. **Do not use a P.O. box number.**		
	City or town, state or province, and country. Include ZIP code or postal code where appropriate.		
3 Mailing address (if different from above)	Street address, apartment number, P.O. box number, or rural route number.		
	City or town, state or province, and country. Include ZIP code or postal code where appropriate.		
4 Birth information	Date of birth (month, day, year) / /	Country of birth	City and state or province (optional) — **5** ☐ Male ☐ Female
6 Family information (see instructions)	Father's last name (surname)	First name	Middle name
	Mother's maiden name (surname)	First name	Middle name
7 Other information	7a Country(ies) of citizenship	7b Foreign tax identification number	7c Type of U.S. visa (if any) and expiration date

7d Describe identification document(s) submitted (see instructions).
☐ Passport ☐ Driver's license/State I.D. ☐ INS documentation ☐ Other
Issued by: Number:

7e Have you previously received a U.S. temporary Taxpayer Identification Number (TIN) or Employer Identification Number (EIN)?
☐ **No/Do not know.** Skip line 7f.
☐ **Yes.** Complete line 7f. If you need more space, list on a sheet and attach to this form. (See instructions.)

7f **TIN** ☐☐☐-☐☐-☐☐☐☐ **EIN** ☐☐-☐☐☐☐☐☐☐
Enter the name under which the TIN was issued. | Enter the name under which the EIN was issued.

Sign Here

Under penalties of perjury, I (applicant/delegate/acceptance agent) declare that I have examined this application, including accompanying documentation and statements, and to the best of my knowledge and belief, it is true, correct, and complete. I authorize the IRS to disclose to my acceptance agent returns or return information necessary to resolve matters regarding the assignment of my IRS individual taxpayer identification number (ITIN).

▶ Signature of applicant (if delegate, see instructions)	Date (month, day, year) / /	Phone number
▶ Name of delegate, if applicable (type or print)	Delegate's relationship to applicant ▶	☐ Parent ☐ Guardian

Keep a copy of this form for your records.

Acceptance Agent's Use ONLY

▶ Signature	Date (month, day, year) / /	Phone: ( ) FAX: ( )
▶ Name and title (type or print)	Name of company	EIN

For Paperwork Reduction Act Notice, see page 4. Cat. No. 10229L Form **W-7** (Rev. 2-98)

TRUE OR FALSE

ACTIVITY: Write **T** for statements that are true and **F** for statements that are false.

1. ______ The filing status of a person with a small child but no spouse is "single."
2. ______ If you owe taxes you are required to pay them by April 15.
3. ______ An aunt may be considered your dependent even if she doesn't live with you, if she meets all the other requirements.
4. ______ Tips are not considered income that can be taxed.
5. ______ Withholding is money your employer takes from your pay and sends to the government to pay an estimate of your total tax bill.
6. ______ Your federal income taxes are used to help pay for health and education programs.
7. ______ If your employer withheld money from your paycheck, you never have to file a tax return form.
8. ______ Social Security tax is the same as federal income tax.
9. ______ Even if you don't have enough money to pay all your taxes, you should file on time and pay part of your taxes.
10. ______ Only paid workers in a family need Social Security numbers.

CROSSWORD PUZZLE

ACTIVITY: Complete the crossword puzzle.

Down

1. Another word for wages or salaries is __________ .
3. A woman whose husband has died is a __________ .
4. You must file your tax return by the __________ or pay a penalty.
8. The deadline for filing your tax return form is in the month of __________ .

Across

2. The money you pay to the government is income __________ .
5. If you are not married, you are __________ .
6. The W-4 form tells your employer how much money to take out, or __________ , from your pay.
7. The agency responsible for income tax is the __________ .
9. Your young child who lives with you is your __________ .
10. The money you receive for work is one type of __________ .

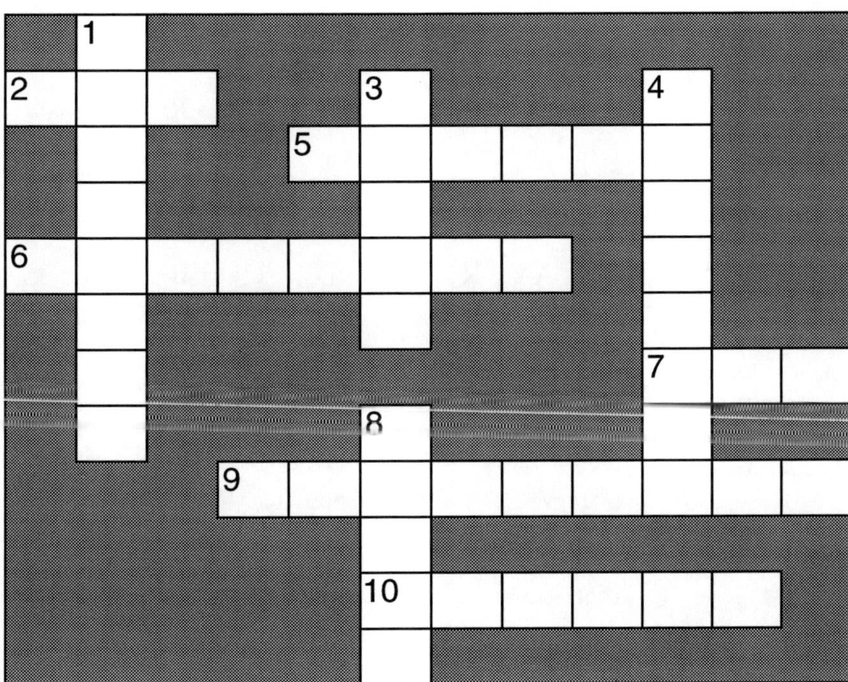

ALPHABET SOUP

Activity: Find the words listed below in the "alphabet soup." They are spelled out vertically (up and down) and horizontally (across). Circle each word that you find.

H P Z Y I W X M D A E T G N O Q
B I J L T K R C S P Z U V K F C
F W A G E S S U P P O R T J Y D
J I U F M E X T E N S I O N P M
O F M D I W E X E M P T I O N X
D E H N Z O P E N A L T Y P G I
H A E I E D E D U C T I O N R L
S T A N D A R D E M E F R C M C
C A D T E N S E P A R A T E L Y
G X O E F S O C I A L W A D M O
W T F R Y J N K X G B I D L A H
A A H E U M A R R I E D K Z T Q
N B O S K T L O N G F O R M N J
E L U T P F K X F V I W E J W Q
T E S I N G L E D L L E P H U K
R S E R E P O R T U E R O C M T
X U H A B I R S G J M Q R D A P
Q M O Y C S S E C U R I T Y Y D
P E L I B R A R Y B C R N C O M
Y L D E P E N D E N T W G J X Z

deduction
dependent
exemption
extension
file
head of household

interest
itemize
library
long form
married
penalty

personal
report
security
separately
single
social

standard
support
tax tables
wages
widower
wife

QUESTIONS

1. If Marilyn Johnson is divorced and has a child living with her, what is her filing status?

2. If Marco Santillana's wife died three years ago, and he has one six-year-old daughter, what is his filing status?

3. Stella and Victor Tran are both 35 years old, are married, and have one child. She earned $5,000 and he earned $15,500. Are they required to file a tax return?

4. Rachel Hollander is 75 and lives alone. Her husband died five years ago. She earned $8,230. Is she required to file a tax return?

5. Bob Deauville is a 17-year-old unmarried high school student. He works part-time at a fast-food restaurant. He earned $4,600. Does he have to file a tax return? If so, what is his filing status? Can he still be claimed as a dependent by his parents?

CHAPTER 5

Filing Procedures

In this chapter, you will learn about:

- Basic filing procedures
- Calculating your total income
- Standard deduction
- Itemized deductions
- IRA deductions
- Exemptions
- Deductions
- Tax tables
- Tax credits
- Forms you need to file your income tax return
- Information you need to fill out the forms
- Review of filing procedure

You will practice filling out forms in the next chapter.

VOCABULARY

ACTIVITY: The definition for each of these words is in the Glossary. As a vocabulary exercise, you may try to write a definition for each word before you look up its meaning in the Glossary.

wages

interest

standard deduction

itemized deduction

exemption

IRA

W-2 form

BASIC FILING PROCEDURES

Listed here are the basic steps you follow when you fill out your tax return form. Each step is explained in the following pages.

1. **Add** up your total income: wages, salary, tips, interest.
2. **Subtract** your deductions: a standard amount or itemized.
3. **Subtract** your exemptions: an amount for you, your spouse, and each dependent.

Once you have subtracted the deductions and exemptions from your total income, you have your **taxable income**.

4. **Use** the tax tables to find how much tax you owe.
5. **Total** your credits and subtract them from the tax you owe. Credits include amounts allotted for child care and credit for elderly or disabled people.
6. **Compare** the amount of tax you owe with the amount of tax withheld by your employer. You will receive a refund or you will owe more taxes.

CALCULATING YOUR INCOME

Add up all your wages, interest, and tips for the year.

- **Your employer must send you a W-2 form indicating how much income you earned for the year and the amount of taxes that were withheld.**

  If you worked for more than one employer, each employer must send you a W-2 form.

  If you worked as an independent contractor, you will receive a 1099 form and not a W-2 form.

  The employer must send you the form by January 31.

  A copy of the form also goes to the IRS.

- **Your bank must send you a 1099-INT form indicating how much interest income you earned for the year.**

  If you have more than one bank, each bank must send you a 1099-INT form.

  The bank must send you the form by January 31

  A copy of the form also goes to the IRS.

SAMPLE INCOME REPORT FORMS: W2 AND 1099-INT

W-2

a Control number	OMB No. 1545-0008	
b Employer identification number	1 Wages, tips, other compensation	2 Federal income tax withheld
c Employer's name, address, and ZIP code	3 Social security wages	4 Social security tax withheld
	5 Medicare wages and tips	6 Medicare tax withheld
	7 Social security tips	8 Allocated tips
d Employee's social security number	9 Advance EIC payment	10 Dependent care benefits
e Employee's name (first, middle initial, last)	11 Nonqualified plans	12 Benefits included in box 1
	13 See instrs. for box 13	14 Other
f Employee's address and ZIP code	15 Statutory employee ☐ Deceased ☐ Pension plan ☐ Legal rep. ☐ Deferred compensation ☐	

16 State Employer's state I.D. no.	17 State wages, tips, etc.	18 State income tax	19 Locality name	20 Local wages, tips, etc.	21 Local income tax

1099-INT

9292 ☐ VOID ☐ CORRECTED

PAYER'S name, street address, city, state, ZIP code, and telephone no.	Payer's RTN (optional)	OMB No. 1545-0112	**Interest Income**
PAYER'S Federal identification number / RECIPIENT'S identification number	1 Interest income not included in box 3 $		**Copy A For Internal Revenue Service Center** File with Form 1096.
RECIPIENT'S name	2 Early withdrawal penalty $	3 Interest on U.S. Savings Bonds and Treas. obligations $	For Privacy Act and Paperwork Reduction Act Notice and instructions for completing this form, see the Instructions for Forms 1099, 1098, 5498, and W-2G.
Street address (including apt. no.)	4 Federal income tax withheld $		
City, state, and ZIP code	5 Foreign tax paid $	6 Foreign country or U.S. possession	
Account number (optional) / 2nd TIN Not. ☐			

Form **1099-INT** 36-2515832 IRS APP. Department of the Treasury - Internal Revenue Service

SAMPLE INCOME REPORT FORMS: W-2

A. W-2 for Joe Hernandez

a Control number		OMB No. 1545-0008
b Employer identification number 9511234567	**1** Wages, tips, other compensation 15,000.00	**2** Federal income tax withheld 1,638.00
c Employer's name, address, and ZIP code Quality Construction Labor Drive Impuesto, CA 90000	**3** Social security wages 15,000.00	**4** Social security tax withheld 930.00
	5 Medicare wages and tips 15,000.00	**6** Medicare tax withheld 217.50
	7 Social security tips 0	**8** Allocated tips
d Employee's social security number 123-45-6789	**9** Advance EIC payment	**10** Dependent care benefits
e Employee's name (first, middle initial, last) Joe Hernandez 300 Primavera Street APT A Impuesto, CA 90000	**11** Nonqualified plans	**12** Benefits included in box 1
	13 See instrs. for box 13	**14** Other
f Employee's address and ZIP code	**15** Statutory employee ☐ Deceased ☐ Pension plan ☐ Legal rep. ☐ Deferred compensation ☐	

16 State	Employer's state I.D. no.	**17** State wages, tips, etc.	**18** State income tax	**19** Locality name	**20** Local wages, tips, etc.	**21** Local income tax
CA		15,000.00	259.77		15,000.00	195.09

B. W-2 for Kim Tranh

a Control number		OMB No. 1545-0008
b Employer identification number 9517654321	**1** Wages, tips, other compensation 7,600.00	**2** Federal income tax withheld 208.00
c Employer's name, address, and ZIP code Cathy's Cafe Main Street Midville, TX 70000	**3** Social security wages 7,600.00	**4** Social security tax withheld 4
	5 Medicare wages and tips 7,600.00	**6** Medicare tax withheld 110.20
	7 Social security tips	**8** Allocated tips
d Employee's social security number 987-65-4321	**9** Advance EIC payment	**10** Dependent care benefits
e Employee's name (first, middle initial, last) Kim Tranh 4300 Lakeview Avenue Midville, TX 70000	**11** Nonqualified plans	**12** Benefits included in box 1
	13 See instrs. for box 13	**14** Other
f Employee's address and ZIP code	**15** Statutory employee ☐ Deceased ☐ Pension plan ☐ Legal rep. ☐ Deferred compensation ☐	

16 State	Employer's state I.D. no.	**17** State wages, tips, etc.	**18** State income tax	**19** Locality name	**20** Local wages, tips, etc.	**21** Local income tax
TX		7,600.00	52.00		7,600.00	48.80

W-2 FORM ACTIVITY

ACTIVITY: Look at the sample W-2 forms. If you have a copy of your own W-2, use it also. For each one, fill in each of the items listed in the first column.

Item	W-2 Form A	W-2 Form B	Your W-2
Federal income tax			
State income tax			
Social Security tax			
Medicare tax			
Wages, tips earned			
Other withholding			

DEDUCTIONS

Deductions are subtracted from your total income to reduce your taxable income. There are two basic kinds of deductions:

- **Standard deduction.**

  A fixed amount that is different for each filing status.

- **Itemized deduction.**

  A variable amount that you calculate according to IRS rules.

STANDARD DEDUCTION

Standard deduction

An amount that you can subtract from the income on which you are taxed. Tax year 1998 standard deductions were:

☐ $4,250 for single people.

☐ $7,100 for married people filing jointly or for a widow(er) with a dependent child.

☐ $3,550 for a married person filing separately.

☐ $6,250 for a head of household.

People who are 65 or older, or who are blind, receive a higher standard deduction.

If you are a nonresident of the United States, you cannot use the standard deduction unless you are married to a U.S. citizen.

ITEMIZED DEDUCTIONS

Some people should itemize their deductions. This means they must use the "long form," Form 1040, for their tax return.

You should itemize if your deductions add up to more than the standard deduction you are allowed.

Deductions you can itemize include:

☐ Mortgage interest you paid on your home.

☐ A portion of medical and dental expenses you paid (not paid back to you by insurance).

☐ Taxes you paid (for example, state income tax and property taxes).

☐ Gifts to charity.

☐ Job expenses your employer did not pay for (such as union dues).

You must keep very good records if you itemize your deductions.

You must be very careful to follow the IRS rules about what is a deduction and what is not.

Use the standard deduction if it is more than the total of the itemized deductions you can claim.

IRA DEDUCTIONS

There is another kind of deduction you can take in addition to the standard or itemized deductions:

- IRA (individual retirement arrangement).

If you have taxable income for the year, you may be able to save and deduct up to $2,000 in a special IRA savings account. This depends on certain conditions, such as your income level and whether you have a retirement plan at work.

- You deduct the money you put in this account from your total income.
- You can't use the money in the IRA account until you are 59½ years old. If you withdraw it sooner, you must pay taxes and penalties.

EXEMPTIONS

Exemptions are subtracted from your total income to reduce your taxable income.

Personal exemptions

- You are allowed one personal exemption for yourself and one for your spouse.
- A personal exemption reduces your taxable income by $2,700.

Dependent exemptions

- You are allowed one exemption for each dependent you claim on your form.
- Each dependent exemption reduces your taxable income by $2,700.
- Each dependent must meet the five specified requirements to qualify for the exemption.

The requirements for a dependent are given in Chapter 4.

TAX TABLES

Once you have figured your taxable income, you can use the tax tables to find the amount of tax you owe.

- Tax tables are provided with the forms.
- You must know your filing status to figure your tax.

Sample tax table

If line 39 (taxable income) is—		And you are—			
At least	But less than	Single	Married filing jointly *	Married filing sepa-rately	Head of a house-hold
		Your tax is—			
17,000					
17,000	**17,050**	2,554	2,554	2,554	2,554
17,050	**17,100**	2,561	2,561	2,561	2,561
17,100	**17,150**	2,569	2,569	2,569	2,569
17,150	**17,200**	2,576	2,576	2,576	2,576
17,200	**17,250**	2,584	2,584	2,584	2,584
17,250	**17,300**	2,591	2,591	2,591	2,591
17,300	**17,350**	2,599	2,599	2,599	2,599
17,350	**17,400**	2,606	2,606	2,606	2,606
17,400	**17,450**	2,614	2,614	2,614	2,614
17,450	**17,500**	2,621	2,621	2,621	2,621
17,500	**17,550**	2,629	2,629	2,629	2,629
17,550	**17,600**	2,636	2,636	2,636	2,636
17,600	**17,650**	2,644	2,644	2,644	2,644
17,650	**17,700**	2,651	2,651	2,651	2,651
17,700	**17,750**	2,659	2,659	2,659	2,659
17,750	**17,800**	2,666	2,666	2,666	2,666
17,800	**17,850**	2,674	2,674	2,674	2,674
17,850	**17,900**	2,681	2,681	2,681	2,681
17,900	**17,950**	2,689	2,689	2,689	2,689
17,950	**18,000**	2,696	2,696	2,696	2,696

TAX TABLE EXERCISE

ACTIVITY: Complete the tax table exercise.

Mary Wong is single. She has one six-year-old child. She calculated her taxable income as $17,942 for 1998.

1. What is her filing status? ______________________________

2. Refer to the tax table to determine how much her tax is. Write the amount here:

____

TAX CREDITS

A tax credit is an amount you can subtract from the amount of taxes you owe. Two examples of tax credits are described in what follows.

Child and dependent care credit

You can receive a credit of up to 30% of your expenses if you pay someone to care for:

- Your dependent under age 13.
- Your disabled spouse or other dependent.

You can get this credit if you are working. If you are looking for work, you may also receive this credit, but you must have an income during the year.

Credit for the elderly or the disabled

A credit is available for persons within certain income limits who are:

- 65 or older.
- Under 65 but retired on permanent and total disability and had taxable disability income.

BASIC TAX CALCULATION EXERCISE

> **Activity:** Complete the tax calculation exercise. Use the tax tables found at the back of this book.

Joe Hernandez is single and has no dependents. He earned $15,000 from one job and $3,500 from another job. His savings account at the bank earned $200 in interest. He has about $1,000 in deductions. He had $2,013 withheld from his pay. Please calculate the following:

1. **Total income** __________

   (Wages + interest)

2. **Deductions** __________

   (Write the larger of standard or itemized deductions.)

3. **Exemptions** __________

   (Number of exemptions × $2,700)

Taxable income __________

(Subtract lines 2 and 3 from line 1.)

---

4. **Taxes owed** __________

   (Refer to the tax tables. Look up the taxable income under the correct column for Joe's filing status. Write the amount of taxes he owes.)

---

5. **Joe is not eligible for any credits, so nothing is subtracted from the taxes owed.**

---

6. **Will he receive a refund, or does he have to pay more taxes?**
   (Compare the amount in line 4 with the amount withheld.)

   Amount withheld __________

   ____

   ☐ How much? __________

WHAT FORM DO YOU NEED?

Short forms

☐ **1040-EZ**

Very short.

Uses the standard deduction.

"Single" or "married filing jointly" filing status only.

For very simple tax situations.

☐ **1040A**

Short.

Uses the standard deduction.

For any filing status.

For simple tax situations.

Long form

☐ **1040**

Long.

May itemize deductions or use standard deduction.

For any filing status.

For more complex tax situations.

WHERE DO YOU GET THE FORMS?

There are many ways to obtain the forms.

- **Mail**

  If you filed last year and live at the same address, you will receive forms in the mail.

- **Post office**
- **Public library**
- **Bank**
- **Local IRS office**
- **Telephone:** 1-800 829 3676 (1-800-TAX-FORM)
- **The Internet:** www.irs.ustreas.gov

SUMMARY OF INFORMATION

The following is a summary of information you need before you begin to fill out your tax return forms.

- Social Security numbers for you, your spouse, and your dependents one year old or older.
- W-2 form(s) from your employer(s).
- 1099-MISC forms if you were self-employed.
- 1099-INT form(s) from your bank(s).
- Receipts and records of deductions if you plan to itemize.

REVIEW OF FILING PROCEDURES

1. **Add** up your total income.
2. **Subtract** your deductions.
3. **Subtract** your exemptions.
   Once you have subtracted the deductions and exemptions, you have your taxable income.
4. **Use** the tax tables to find out how much tax you owe.
5. **Total** your credits and subtract them from the tax you owe.
6. **Compare** the tax you owe with the tax withheld from your paycheck to determine if you receive a refund or if you owe more taxes.

CHAPTER 6

Filling Out Forms—1040EZ

In this chapter, you will practice filling out the simplest income tax form:

- 1040EZ

You will use information provided about a sample taxpayer, and/or information about your own situation.

VOCABULARY

ACTIVITY: The definition for each of these words is in the Glossary. As a vocabulary exercise, you may try to write a definition for each word before you look up its meaning in the Glossary.

sighted

taxable income

claim

dividends

tax-exempt

INSTRUCTIONS

- Read the information about Joe Hernandez, the sample taxpayer.
- Read the explanation of the 1040EZ form in this chapter.
- Complete the form using the information about the sample taxpayer.

1040EZ PRACTICE EXERCISE

ACTIVITY: Fill out the 1040EZ form for Joe Hernandez. The next sections in this chapter have step-by-step instructions.

Joe Hernandez is a carpenter. He is single and has no dependents.

He earned $15,000 from one job and later earned $3,500 from another job.

His savings account at the bank earned $200 in interest. He has about $1,000 in deductions.

He has a total of $2,013 withheld from his pay.

He lives at 300 Primavera Street, Apt. A, Impuesto, CA 90000. His Social Security number is 123-45-6789, and he would like to contribute to the Presidential Election Campaign fund.

W-2 FORM—JOE HERNANDEZ

a Control number	OMB No. 1545-0008	
b Employer identification number 9511234567	**1** Wages, tips, other compensation 15,000.00	**2** Federal income tax withheld 1,638.00
c Employer's name, address, and ZIP code Quality Construction Labor Drive Impuesto, CA 90000	**3** Social security wages 15,000.00	**4** Social security tax withheld 930.00
	5 Medicare wages and tips 15,000.00	**6** Medicare tax withheld 217.50
	7 Social security tips 0	**8** Allocated tips
d Employee's social security number 123-45-6789	**9** Advance EIC payment	**10** Dependent care benefits
e Employee's name (first, middle initial, last) Joe Hernandez 300 Primavera Street APT A Impuesto, CA 90000	**11** Nonqualified plans	**12** Benefits included in box 1
	13 See instrs. for box 13	**14** Other
f Employee's address and ZIP code	**15** Statutory employee ☐ Deceased ☐ Pension plan ☐ Legal rep. ☐ Deferred compensation ☐	

16 State	Employer's state I.D. no.	**17** State wages, tips, etc.	**18** State income tax	**19** Locality name	**20** Local wages, tips, etc.	**21** Local income tax
		15,000.00	259.77		15,000.00	195.09

WHO CAN USE THE 1040EZ?

- You can use the 1040EZ if you meet the following requirements:
  - ☐ Sighted single person or married couple filing jointly and under 65.
  - ☐ Total taxable income of $50,000 or less.
  - ☐ Taxable interest income of $400 or less.
  - ☐ Uses standard deduction, May NOT itemize deductions.
  - ☐ No dependents.
  - ☐ U.S. resident.
  - ☐ All taxable income comes from earnings reported on W-2 and interest (no rental income or income from own business).

ACTIVITY: Can Joe Hernandez use the 1040EZ? Why or why not?

1040EZ—SIDE 1

Form **1040EZ**

Department of the Treasury—Internal Revenue Service

Income Tax Return for Single and Joint Filers With No Dependents (99) **1998** OMB No. 1545-0675

Use the IRS label here

Your first name and initial | Last name

If a joint return, spouse's first name and initial | Last name

Home address (number and street). If you have a P.O. box, see page 7. | Apt. no.

City, town or post office, state, and ZIP code. If you have a foreign address, see page 7.

Your social security number

Spouse s social security number

▲ IMPORTANT! ▲ You **must** enter your SSN(s) above.

Presidential Election Campaign (See page 7.)

Note: *Checking Yes will not change your tax or reduce your refund.*

Do you want $3 to go to this fund? ▶ Yes ☐ No ☐

If a joint return, does your spouse want $3 to go to this fund? ▶ Yes ☐ No ☐

Dollars **Cents**

Income

Attach Copy B of Form(s) W-2 here. Enclose, but do not staple, any payment.

1 Total wages, salaries, and tips. This should be shown in box 1 of your W-2 form(s). Attach your W-2 form(s). 1

2 Taxable interest income. If the total is over $400, you cannot use Form 1040EZ. 2

3 Unemployment compensation (see page 8). 3

4 Add lines 1, 2, and 3. This is your **adjusted gross income.** If under $10,030, see page 9 to find out if you can claim the earned income credit on line 8a. 4

Note: *You **must** check Yes or No.*

5 Can your parents (or someone else) claim you on their return?
Yes. ☐ Enter amount from worksheet on back.
No. ☐ If **single,** enter 6,950.00. If **married,** enter 12,500.00. See back for explanation. 5

6 Subtract line 5 from line 4. If line 5 is larger than line 4, enter 0. This is your **taxable income.** ▶ 6

Payments and tax

7 Enter your Federal income tax withheld from box 2 of your W-2 form(s). 7

8a **Earned income credit** (see page 9).
b Nontaxable earned income: enter type and amount below.
Type | $ 8a

9 Add lines 7 and 8a. These are your **total payments.** 9

10 **Tax.** Use the amount on **line 6 above** to find your tax in the tax table on pages 20—24 of the booklet. Then, enter the tax from the table on this line. 10

Refund

Have it directly deposited! See page 12 and fill in 11b, 11c, and 11d.

11a If line 9 is larger than line 10, subtract line 10 from line 9. This is your **refund.** 11a

▶ **b** Routing number

▶ **c** Type: Checking ☐ Savings ☐

d Account number

Amount you owe

12 If line 10 is larger than line 9, subtract line 9 from line 10. This is the **amount you owe.** See page 14 for details on how to pay. 12

I have read this return. Under penalties of perjury, I declare that to the best of my knowledge and belief, the return is true, correct, and accurately lists all amounts and sources of income I received during the tax year.

Sign here ▶ Keep copy for your records.

Your signature | Spouse s signature if joint return. See page 7.

Date | Your occupation | Date | Spouse s occupation

For Official Use Only 1 2 3 4 5 6 7 8 9 10

For Disclosure, Privacy Act, and Paperwork Reduction Act Notice, see page 18. Cat. No. 11329W 1998 Form 1040EZ

1040EZ—SIDE 2

1998 Form 1040EZ page 2

Use this form if

- Your filing status is single or married filing jointly.
- You (and your spouse if married) were under 65 on January 1, 1999, and not blind at the end of 1998.
- You do not claim any dependents.
- Your taxable income (line 6) is less than $50,000.
- You do not claim a student loan interest deduction or an education credit. See page 3.
- You had only wages, salaries, tips, taxable scholarship or fellowship grants, unemployment compensation, or Alaska Permanent Fund dividends, and your taxable interest income was not over $400. But if you earned tips, including allocated tips, that are not included in box 5 and box 7 of your W-2, you may not be able to use Form 1040EZ. See page 8.
- You did not receive any advance earned income credit payments.

If you are not sure about your filing status, see page 7. If you have questions about dependents, use TeleTax topic 354 (see page 17). If you cannot use this form, use TeleTax topic 352 (see page 17).

Filling in your return

For tips on how to avoid common mistakes, see page 25.

Enter your (and your spouse s if married) social security number on the front. Because this form is read by a machine, please print your numbers inside the boxes like this:

9 8 7 6 5 4 3 2 1 0   Do not type your numbers. Do not use dollar signs.

If you received a scholarship or fellowship grant or tax-exempt interest income, such as on municipal bonds, see the booklet before filling in the form. Also, see the booklet if you received a Form 1099-INT showing Federal income tax withheld or if Federal income tax was withheld from your unemployment compensation or Alaska Permanent Fund dividends.

Remember, you must report all wages, salaries, and tips even if you do not get a W-2 form from your employer. You must also report all your taxable interest income, including interest from banks, savings and loans, credit unions, etc., even if you do not get a Form 1099-INT.

Worksheet for dependents who checked "Yes" on line 5

Use this worksheet to figure the amount to enter on line 5 if someone can claim you (or your spouse if married) as a dependent, even if that person chooses not to do so. To find out if someone can claim you as a dependent, use TeleTax topic 354 (see page 17).

A. Amount, if any, from line 1 on front ______
+ 250.00 Enter total ► A. ______

B. Minimum standard deduction . . . . B. 700.00

C. Enter the LARGER of line A or line B here . . . . C. ______

D. Maximum standard deduction. If single, enter 4,250.00; if married, enter 7,100.00 . . . . D. ______

E. Enter the SMALLER of line C or line D here. This is your standard deduction . . . . E. ______

F. Exemption amount.
- If single, enter 0.
- If married and
  both you and your spouse can be claimed as dependents, enter 0.
  only one of you can be claimed as a dependent, enter 2,700.00.

F. ______

G. Add lines E and F. Enter the total here and on line 5 on the front . . G. ______

If you checked No on line 5 because no one can claim you (or your spouse if married) as a dependent, enter on line 5 the amount shown below that applies to you.

- Single, enter 6,950.00. This is the total of your standard deduction (4,250.00) and your exemption (2,700.00).
- Married, enter 12,500.00. This is the total of your standard deduction (7,100.00), your exemption (2,700.00), and your spouse s exemption (2,700.00).

Mailing return

Mail your return by April 15, 1999. Use the envelope that came with your booklet. If you do not have that envelope, see page 28 for the address to use.

Paid preparer's use only

See page 14.

Under penalties of perjury, I declare that I have examined this return, and to the best of my knowledge and belief, it is true, correct, and accurately lists all amounts and sources of income received during the tax year. This declaration is based on all information of which I have any knowledge.

Preparer s signature ►	Date	Check if self-employed ☐	Preparer s SSN
Firm s name (or yours if self-employed) and address ►		EIN	
		ZIP code	

SECTION 1: NAME AND ADDRESS

In this initial section of the 1040EZ form, you print personal information.

Form **1040EZ**

Department of the Treasury—Internal Revenue Service
Income Tax Return for Single and Joint Filers With No Dependents (99) **1998** OMB No. 1545-0675

Use the IRS label here	
	Your first name and initial — Last name
	If a joint return, spouse's first name and initial — Last name
	Home address (number and street). If you have a P.O. box, see page 7. — Apt. no.
	City, town or post office, state, and ZIP code. If you have a foreign address, see page 7.

Your social security number

Spouse's social security number

▲ **IMPORTANT!** ▲
You **must** enter your SSN(s) above.

Presidential Election Campaign (See page 7.)

Note: *Checking "Yes" will not change your tax or reduce your refund.*

Do you want $3 to go to this fund? ▶ **Yes** ☐ **No** ☐

If a joint return, does your spouse want $3 to go to this fund? ▶ **Yes** ☐ **No** ☐

- **In the large rectangle, print your and your spouse's:**

  First name, initial, and last (family) name.

  Home address: number, street, and apartment number.

  City, state, and ZIP code.

- **In the boxes to the right of the large rectangle, print your and your spouse's Social Security numbers.**

Presidential election campaign contribution

In this section, you must decide whether you want the IRS to contribute $3.00 of your tax money to a special fund to help pay for presidential election costs. This will not increase your tax owed or decrease the amount of your refund. The money the IRS contributes to this fund is money that you have already paid.

- Mark an X in the first Yes box if you do want the IRS to contribute $3.00 to the special fund. Or mark an X in the first No box if you do *not* want the IRS to contribute $3.00 to the special fund.
- Mark an X in the second Yes box if your spouse does want the IRS to contribute $3.00 to the special fund. Or mark an X in the second No box if your spouse does *not* want the IRS to contribute $3.00 to the special fund.

SECTION 2: REPORTING YOUR INCOME

In this section of the 1040EZ, you print financial information. You must also indicate whether your parents (or anyone else) can claim you as a dependent on their income tax return.

Income			Dollars	Cents
Attach Copy B of Form(s) W-2 here. Enclose, but do not staple, any payment.	**1**	Total wages, salaries, and tips. This should be shown in box 1 of your W-2 form(s). Attach your W-2 form(s). 1	□□,□□□	.□□
	2	Taxable interest income. If the total is over $400, you cannot use Form 1040EZ. 2	□□□	.□□
	3	Unemployment compensation (see page 8). 3	□□,□□□	.□□
	4	Add lines 1, 2, and 3. This is your **adjusted gross income.** If under $10,030, see page 9 to find out if you can claim the earned income credit on line 8a. 4	□□,□□□	.□□
Note: *You* ***must*** *check Yes or No.*	**5**	Can your parents (or someone else) claim you on their return? **Yes.** □ Enter amount from worksheet on back. **No.** □ If **single,** enter 6,950.00. If **married,** enter 12,500.00. See back for explanation. 5	□□,□□□	.□□
	6	Subtract line 5 from line 4. If line 5 is larger than line 4, enter 0. This is your **taxable income.** ► 6	□□,□□□	.□□

1. Add up wages, salaries, and tips. Print the total in the boxes to the right of 1.
2. Add up total interest income. Print the total in the boxes to the right of 2.
3. Add up unemployment compensation. Print the total in the boxes to the right of 3.
4. Add lines 1, 2, and 3. Print this total in the boxes to the right of 4.
5. Mark an X:

   - In the Yes box if your parents (or someone else) can claim you as a dependent on their income tax report.

   If you mark the Yes box, you must complete the standard deduction worksheet, which follows, and print the amount from line G in the boxes on the right.

   - In the No box if no one claims you as a dependent on their income tax report.

   If you mark the No box, print $6,950.00 if you are single or $12,500.00 if you are married filing together in the boxes to the right of 5.

6. Subtract the amount on line 5 from the amount on line 4 (line 4 – line 5).

   - Print the result in the boxes to the right of 6.
   - If 5 is larger than 4, print 0 in the boxes to the right of 6.
   - This amount is your taxable income.

STANDARD DEDUCTION WORKSHEET

This worksheet is only for those who marked an X in the Yes box in 5. You can find the worksheet on the back of form 1040EZ. If you marked No in 5, go to the next page.

Worksheet for dependents who checked "Yes" on line 5

Use this worksheet to figure the amount to enter on line 5 if someone can claim you (or your spouse if married) as a dependent, even if that person chooses not to do so. To find out if someone can claim you as a dependent, use TeleTax topic 354 (see page 17).

A. Amount, if any, from line 1 on front ______
+ 250.00 Enter total ▶ A. ______

B. Minimum standard deduction . . . . B. 700.00

C. Enter the LARGER of line A or line B here . . . . C. ______

D. Maximum standard deduction. If single, enter 4,250.00; if married, enter 7,100.00 . . . . D. ______

E. Enter the SMALLER of line C or line D here. This is your standard deduction . . . . E. ______

F. Exemption amount.
- If single, enter 0.
- If married and
  both you and your spouse can be claimed as dependents, enter 0.
  only one of you can be claimed as a dependent, enter 2,700.00.

F. ______

G. Add lines E and F. Enter the total here and on line 5 on the front . . G. ______

If you checked No on line 5 because no one can claim you (or your spouse if married) as a dependent, enter on line 5 the amount shown below that applies to you.

- Single, enter 6,950.00. This is the total of your standard deduction (4,250.00) and your exemption (2,700.00).
- Married, enter 12,500.00. This is the total of your standard deduction (7,100.00), your exemption (2,700.00), and your spouse s exemption (2,700.00).

- On line A, add the amount from line 1 to $250.00.
- On line C, print the larger number:

  Either the total income (line A)

  OR

  $700.00 (line B).
- On line D, print $4,250.00 if you are single or $7,100.00 if you are married filing together.
- On line E, print the smaller number:

  Either the amount on line C

  OR

  The amount on line D.
- On line F, print the exemption amount ($0 or $2,700.00).
- On line G, add the amounts on lines E and F.

  Write the line G number on line 5 on the 1040EZ.

SECTION 3: FIGURING YOUR TAX

In this section of the 1040EZ, you figure the amount of income tax already withheld from paychecks. Then you look in the Tax Tables to find out how much tax is owed.

Payments and tax

7 Enter your Federal income tax withheld from box 2 of your W-2 form(s). 7

8a **Earned income credit** (see page 9).
b Nontaxable earned income: enter type and amount below.
Type | $ 8a

9 Add lines 7 and 8a. These are your **total payments.** 9

10 **Tax.** Use the amount on **line 6 above** to find your tax in the tax table on pages 20–24 of the booklet. Then, enter the tax from the table on this line. 10

7. Look at box 2 of the W-2 form to find the total federal income tax withheld. If you have more than one W-2 form, add the amounts from each one.

   Print the total federal income tax withheld in the boxes to the right of 7.

8. If your (and your spouse's) income is less than $10,030, you may be eligible to receive a special credit—called the earned income credit.

   To receive this credit, you must fulfill the following four requirements:

   - you (and your spouse) must be at least 25 years old, but under the age of 65 in 1998
   - you (and your spouse) cannot be claimed as a dependent on someone else's 1998 income tax (see 5, earlier)
   - you (and your spouse) must have lived in the United States for more than six months in 1998
   - you (can your spouse) received less than $10,030 of taxable and nontaxable earned income in 1998

8a. If you fulfill these four requirements, print EIC in the space to the right of the word "below" on line 8b. The IRS will calculate this credit for you.

8b. Certain types of income are not taxable but you must include them on your 1040EZ to see if you qualify to receive the earned income tax credit. Examples of nontaxable earned income are housing allowances or meals and lodging provided by your employer or the military.

NOTE: Welfare, SSI, and Food Stamps are NOT earned income. Do not include them in 8b.

If you received nontaxable earned income, write the type and the amount on 8b.

If you are eligible for the earned income credit, leave the rest of the 1040EZ blank, except for your (and your spouse's) signature.

If you are NOT eligible for the earned income credit, write 0 in the boxes to the right of 8a and continue to complete this form; lines 9 to 12.

9. Add the amounts on line 7 and line 8a. These are your **total payments.**

10. Look in the Tax Tables and find the taxable income you wrote on line 6. Then find in the tax table how much tax you owe on the line 6 amount.

    Print the amount of your tax in the boxes to the right of 10.

SECTION 4: REFUND OR TAXES OWED

In this section of the 1040EZ, you must compare the amount of money withheld from paychecks with the amount of taxes listed in the tax tables.

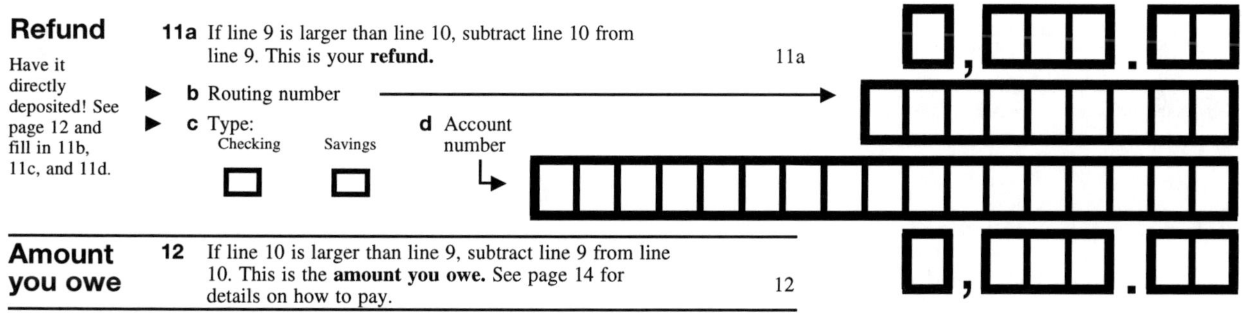

Refund
Have it directly deposited! See page 12 and fill in 11b, 11c, and 11d.

11a If line 9 is larger than line 10, subtract line 10 from line 9. This is your **refund.** 11a

▶ **b** Routing number

▶ **c** Type: Checking Savings **d** Account number

Amount you owe
12 If line 10 is larger than line 9, subtract line 9 from line 10. This is the **amount you owe.** See page 14 for details on how to pay. 12

11a. Look at the amount on line 9. If it is larger than the amount on line 10, subtract 10 from 9 (line 9 – line 10).

     Print the result in the boxes to the right of 11a.

     You have paid too much in taxes and you will receive a refund.

     The IRS will now directly deposit your refund in the bank if you have a checking or savings account. This is a good idea because it prevents lost or stolen income tax refund checks. If you prefer to receive a refund check, leave 11b, 11c, and 11d blank.

11b. Print the routing number of your bank. (Ask the bank for this nine-digit number.)

11c. Put an X in the correct box to indicate whether your income tax refund is to be deposited into your checking or savings account.

11d. Write your account number in the boxes.

12. If the amount on line 9 is smaller than the amount on line 10, then subtract 9 from 10 (line 10 – line 9).

    Print the result in the boxes to the right of 12. (Line 11a will remain blank.)

    You owe this amount of taxes to the IRS.

    Prepare a check or money order payable to the IRS for this amount.

    Print your name, address, Social Security number, daytime telephone number, and "199_ Form 1040EZ" on the check or money order.

SECTION 5: SIGNATURE

In this final section of the 1040EZ, you must sign and date your income tax report.

I have read this return. Under penalties of perjury, I declare that to the best of my knowledge and belief, the return is true, correct, and accurately lists all amounts and sources of income I received during the tax year.

Sign here	Your signature		Spouse s signature if joint return. See page 7.	
Keep copy for your records.	Date	Your occupation	Date	Spouse s occupation

For Official Use Only: 1 2 3 4 5 / 6 7 8 9 10

For Disclosure, Privacy Act, and Paperwork Reduction Act Notice, see page 18. Cat. No. 11329W 1998 Form 1040EZ

- Sign your name.
- Print the date on the line below your signature. If you are married, your spouse also needs to sign, date, and write his or her occupation.
- Beside the date, write what your occupation is.

1040EZ FINAL PROCEDURES

- ☐ Make a copy of the tax return for your records.
- ☐ Staple Copy B of your W-2 form(s) to the original 1040EZ form.
- ☐ If you owe taxes, staple your check or money order, on top of the W-2 form(s), to the original 1040EZ form.
- ☐ Send Copy B of the W-2 form(s) and the original 1040EZ, plus any payment, to the Internal Revenue Service Center. Select the address from the list at the end of this chapter.

YOUR 1040EZ

If you wish to complete a 1040EZ form for yourself, remember that the forms and amounts in this book are not for the current year.

Fill out the forms in this book for practice, but use a current form and the amounts on that form when you prepare your taxes.

Information on where to get help is in Chapter 8.

IRS CENTERS

Alabama—Memphis, TN 37501
Alaska—Ogden, UT 84201
Arizona—Ogden, UT 84201
Arkansas—Memphis, TN 37501
California—*Counties of Alpine, Amador, Butts, Calaveras, Colusa, Contra Costa, Del Norte, El Dorado, Glenn, Humboldt, Lake, Lassen, Marin, Mendocino, Modoc, Napa, Nevada, Placer, Plumas, Sacramento, San Joaquin, Shasta, Sierra, Siskiyou, Solano, Sonoma, Sutter, Tehama, Trinity, Yolo, and Yuba*—Ogden, UT 84201
All other counties—Fresno, CA 93888
Colorado—Ogden, UT 84201
Connecticut—Andover, MA 05501
Delaware—Philadelphia, PA 19255
District of Columbia—Philadelphia, PA 19255
Florida—Atlanta, GA 39901
Georgia—Atlanta, GA 39901
Hawaii—Fresno, CA 93888
Idaho—Ogden, UT 84201
Illinois—Kansas City, MO 64999
Indiana—Cincinnati, OH 45999
Iowa—Kansas City, MO 64999
Kansas—Austin, TX 73301
Kentucky—Cincinnati, OH 45999
Louisiana—Memphis, TN 37501
Maine—Andover, MA 05501
Maryland—Philadelphia, PA 19255
Massachusetts—Andover, MA 05501
Michigan—Cincinnati, OH 45999
Minnesota—Kansas City, MO 64999
Mississippi—Memphis, TN 37501
Missouri—Kansas City, MO 64999
Montana—Ogden, UT 84201
Nebraska—Ogden, UT 84201
Nevada—Ogden, UT 84201
New Hampshire—Andover, MA 05501
New Jersey—Holtsville, NY 00501
New Mexico—Austin, TX 73301
New York—*New York City and counties of Nassau, Rockland, Suffolk, and Westchester*—Holtsville, NY 00501
All other counties—Andover, MA 05501
North Carolina—Memphis, TN 37501
North Dakota—Ogden, UT 84201
Ohio—Cincinnati, OH 45999
Oklahoma—Austin, TX 73301
Oregon—Ogden, UT 84201
Pennsylvania—Philadelphia, PA 19255
Rhode Island—Andover, MA 05501
South Carolina—Atlanta, GA 39901
South Dakota—Ogden, UT 84201
Tennessee—Memphis, TN 37501
Texas—Austin, TX 73301
Utah—Ogden, UT 84201
Vermont—Andover, MA 05501
Virginia—Philadelphia, PA 19255
Washington—Ogden, UT 84201
West Virginia—Cincinnati, OH 45999
Wisconsin—Kansas City, MO 64999
Wyoming—Ogden, UT 84201
American Samoa—Philadelphia, PA 19255
Guam—Commissioner of Revenue and Taxation
855 West Marine Dr.
Agana, GU 96910
Puerto Rico *(or if excluding income under section 933)*—Philadelphia, PA 19255
Virgin Islands: Nonpermanent residents—
Philadelphia, PA 19255
Virgin Islands: Permanent residents—
V.I. Bureau of Internal Revenue
Lockharts Garden No. 1A
Charlotte Amalie
St. Thomas, VI 00802
Foreign country: *U.S. citizens and those filing Form 2555, Form 2555-EZ, or Form 4563*—
Philadelphia, PA 19255
All A.P.O. and F.P.O. addresses—
Philadelphia, PA 19255

CHAPTER 7

Filling Out Forms—1040A

In this chapter, you will practice filling out the other simple income tax form:

- 1040A

You will use information provided about a sample taxpayer and/or information about your own situation.

INSTRUCTIONS

- Read the information about the first sample taxpayer, Kim Tranh.
- Read the explanation of the 1040A form in this chapter.
- Complete the form for the first sample taxpayer using the information in the practice exercise.
- Complete the form for the other sample taxpayers using the information in the practice exercises at the end of this chapter.

COMPLETING THE 1040A—EXERCISE 1

ACTIVITY: Fill out the form for Kim Tranh's family. The next sections in this chapter have step-by-step instructions.

Kim Tranh is a part-time waitress. Her husband, Viet, is a medical technician. Their daughter, Sun, is seven years old, and their son, Lee, is four.

Viet earned $24,800, and Kim earned $7,600, including tips.

They have no savings, and they have $2,500 in deductions.

Viet had $2,080 withheld from his pay, and Kim had $208 withheld from her pay.

They are not eligible to receive the earned income credit.

The Social Security numbers for the family are:

Kim:	987-65-4321
Viet:	001-34-3445
Sun:	002-22-9998
Lee:	002-45-9834

They live at 4300 Lakeview Avenue, Midville, TX 70000. They want to contribute to the Presidential Election Campaign fund.

1040A—PAGE 1

Form **1040A** — Department of the Treasury–Internal Revenue Service
U.S. Individual Income Tax Return **1998** — IRS Use Only–Do not write or staple in this space.

OMB No. 1545-0085

Label (See page 18.)

Use the IRS label. Otherwise, please print or type.

LABEL HERE

Your first name and initial	Last name	**Your social security number**
If a joint return, spouse's first name and initial	Last name	**Spouse's social security number**
Home address (number and street). If you have a P.O. box, see page 19.	Apt. no.	
City, town or post office, state, and ZIP code. If you have a foreign address, see page 19.		

▲ IMPORTANT! ▲
You **must** enter your SSN(s) above.

Presidential Election Campaign Fund (See page 19.)

	Yes	No
Do you want $3 to go to this fund?		
If a joint return, does your spouse want $3 to go to this fund?		

Note: *Checking "Yes" will not change your tax or reduce your refund.*

Filing status

Check only one box.

1 ☐ Single
2 ☐ Married filing joint return (even if only one had income)
3 ☐ Married filing separate return. Enter spouse's social security number above and full name here. ▶ ____
4 ☐ Head of household (with qualifying person). (See page 20.) If the qualifying person is a child but not your dependent, enter this child's name here. ▶ ____
5 ☐ Qualifying widow(er) with dependent child (year spouse died ▶ 19). (See page 21.)

Exemptions

6a ☐ **Yourself.** If your parent (or someone else) can claim you as a dependent on his or her tax return, **do not** check box 6a.
b ☐ **Spouse**

No. of boxes checked on 6a and 6b ____

c **Dependents:**

If more than seven dependents, see page 21.

(1) First name Last name	(2) Dependent's social security number	(3) Dependent's relationship to you	(4) ✓ if qualified child for child tax credit (see page 22)
			☐
			☐
			☐
			☐
			☐
			☐
			☐

No. of your children on 6c who:
• lived with you ____
• did not live with you due to divorce or separation (see page 23) ____
Dependents on 6c not entered above ____

d Total number of exemptions claimed.

Add numbers entered on lines above ☐

Income

Attach Copy B of your Forms W-2 and 1099-R here.

If you did not get a W-2, see page 24.

Enclose, but do not staple, any payment.

7	Wages, salaries, tips, etc. Attach Form(s) W-2.		7
8a	**Taxable** interest. Attach Schedule 1 if required.		8a
b	**Tax-exempt** interest. DO NOT include on line 8a.	8b	
9	Ordinary dividends. Attach Schedule 1 if required.		9
10a	Total IRA distributions. 10a	**10b** Taxable amount (see page 24).	10b
11a	Total pensions and annuities. 11a	**11b** Taxable amount (see page 25).	11b
12	Unemployment compensation.		12
13a	Social security benefits. 13a	**13b** Taxable amount (see page 27).	13b
14	Add lines 7 through 13b (far right column). This is your **total income.**		▶ 14

Adjusted gross income

15	IRA deduction (see page 28).	15	
16	Student loan interest deduction (see page 28).	16	
17	Add lines 15 and 16. These are your **total adjustments.**		17
18	Subtract line 17 from line 14. This is your **adjusted gross income.** If under $30,095 (under $10,030 if a child did not live with you), see the EIC instructions on page 36.		▶ 18

For Disclosure, Privacy Act, and Paperwork Reduction Act Notice, see page 49. Cat. No. 11327A **1998 Form 1040A**

1040A—PAGE 2

1998 Form 1040A page 2

Taxable income

19 Enter the amount from line 18. 19

20a Check if: ☐ **You** were 65 or older ☐ Blind / ☐ **Spouse** was 65 or older ☐ Blind — **Enter number of boxes checked** ▶ 20a ☐

b If you are married filing separately and your spouse itemizes deductions, see page 30 and check here . . . . . . ▶ 20b ☐

21 Enter the **standard deduction** for your filing status. **But** see page 31 if you checked any box on line 20a or 20b **OR** if someone can claim you as a dependent.
- Single—$4,250
- Married filing jointly or Qualifying widow(er)—$7,100
- Head of household—$6,250
- Married filing separately—$3,550

21

22 Subtract line 21 from line 19. If line 21 is more than line 19, enter -0-. 22

23 Multiply $2,700 by the total number of exemptions claimed on line 6d. 23

24 Subtract line 23 from line 22. If line 23 is more than line 22, enter -0-. This is your **taxable income.** ▶ 24

Tax, credits, and payments

25 Find the tax on the amount on line 24 (see page 31). 25

26 Credit for child and dependent care expenses. Attach Schedule 2. 26

27 Credit for the elderly or the disabled. Attach Schedule 3. 27

28 Child tax credit (see page 32). 28

29 Education credits. Attach Form 8863. 29

30 Adoption credit. Attach Form 8839. 30

31 Add lines 26 through 30. These are your **total credits.** 31

32 Subtract line 31 from line 25. If line 31 is more than line 25, enter -0-. 32

33 Advance earned income credit payments from Form(s) W-2. 33

34 Add lines 32 and 33. This is your **total tax.** ▶ 34

35 Total Federal income tax withheld from Forms W-2 and 1099. 35

36 1998 estimated tax payments and amount applied from 1997 return. 36

37a **Earned income credit.** Attach Schedule EIC if you have a qualifying child. 37a

b Nontaxable earned income: amount ▶ and type ▶

38 Additional child tax credit. Attach Form 8812. 38

39 Add lines 35, 36, 37a, and 38. These are your **total payments.** ▶ 39

Refund

Have it directly deposited! See page 43 and fill in 41b, 41c, and 41d.

40 If line 39 is more than line 34, subtract line 34 from line 39. This is the amount you **overpaid.** 40

41a Amount of line 40 you want **refunded to you.** 41a

b Routing number ☐☐☐☐☐☐☐☐☐ **c** Type: ☐ Checking ☐ Savings

d Account number ☐☐☐☐☐☐☐☐☐☐☐☐☐☐☐☐☐

42 Amount of line 40 you want **applied to your 1999 estimated tax.** 42

Amount you owe

43 If line 34 is more than line 39, subtract line 39 from line 34. This is the **amount you owe.** For details on how to pay, see page 44. 43

44 Estimated tax penalty (see page 44). 44

Sign here

Joint return? See page 19. Keep a copy for your records.

Under penalties of perjury, I declare that I have examined this return and accompanying schedules and statements, and to the best of my knowledge and belief, they are true, correct, and accurately list all amounts and sources of income I received during the tax year. Declaration of preparer (other than the taxpayer) is based on all information of which the preparer has any knowledge.

Your signature	Date	Your occupation	Daytime telephone number (optional)
Spouse's signature. If joint return, BOTH must sign.	Date	Spouse's occupation	( )

Paid preparer's use only

Preparer's signature ▶	Date	Check if self-employed ☐	Preparer's social security no.
Firm's name (or yours if self-employed) and address ▶			EIN
			ZIP code

1040A—CHILD TAX CREDIT WORKSHEET

Child Tax Credit Worksheet–Line 28

▶ Keep for your records.

Do Not File

1. $400.00 ______________ . Multiply and enter the result . . . . 1. ______
Enter number of qualifying children (see page 32)

2. Enter the amount from Form 1040A, line 19 . . . . . . 2. ______

3. Is line 2 above more than $55,000?

☐ **No.** Skip lines 3 through 5, enter -0- on line 6, and go to line 7.

☐ **Yes.** Enter: $75,000 if single, head of household, or qualifying widow(er); $110,000 if married filing jointly; $55,000 if married filing separately . . . . . . 3. ______

4. Subtract line 3 from line 2. If zero or less, enter -0- here and on line 6, and go to line 7 . . . . 4. ______

5. Divide line 4 by $1,000. If the result is not a whole number, round it up to the next higher whole number (for example, round 0.01 to 1) . . . . 5. ______

6. Multiply $50 by the number on line 5 . . . . 6. ______

7. Subtract line 6 from line 1. If zero or less, **stop here;** you **cannot** take this credit . 7. ______

8. Enter the amount from Form 1040A, line 25 . . . . . . 8. ______

9. Is line 1 above more than $800?

☐ **No.** Add the amounts from Form 1040A, lines 26, 27, and 29. Enter the total.

☐ **Yes.** Enter the amount from the worksheet on page 34. } 9. ______

10. Subtract line 9 above from line 8 . . . . 10. ______

11. **Child tax credit.** Enter the **smaller** of line 7 or line 10 here and on Form 1040A, line 28 ▶ 11. ______

TIP *If line 1 above is more than $800, you may be able to take the **Additional Child Tax Credit.** See page 32.*

WHO CAN USE THE 1040A?

The 1040A is for taxpayers of any age with:

☐ A total taxable income of $50,000 or less.

☐ Any amount of taxable interest or dividend income.

☐ Any filing status.

☐ Any number of dependents.

Unacceptable income sources:

☐ Rental income.

☐ Income from own business or contract work.

SECTION 1: NAME AND ADDRESS

In this initial section of the 1040A form, you print personal information.

Form **1040A** Department of the Treasury–Internal Revenue Service **U.S. Individual Income Tax Return** **1998** IRS Use Only–Do not write or staple in this space.

OMB No. 1545-0085

Label (See page 18.) **Use the IRS label.** Otherwise, please print or type.	LABEL HERE	Your first name and initial	Last name		**Your social security number**
		If a joint return, spouse's first name and initial	Last name		**Spouse's social security number**
		Home address (number and street). If you have a P.O. box, see page 19.		Apt. no.	**▲ IMPORTANT! ▲** You **must** enter your SSN(s) above.
		City, town or post office, state, and ZIP code. If you have a foreign address, see page 19.			

Presidential Election Campaign Fund (See page 19.)	**Yes**	**No**	**Note:** *Checking "Yes" will not change your tax or reduce your refund.*
Do you want $3 to go to this fund?			
If a joint return, does your spouse want $3 to go to this fund?			

- In the large rectangle, print:

  Your first name, initial, and last (family) name.

  Your spouse's first name, initial, and last (family) name, if applicable.

  Home address: number, street, and apartment number.

  City, state, and ZIP code.

- To the right of the large rectangle, print your Social Security number. Also print your spouse's Social Security number if you are married.

Presidential election campaign contribution

In this section, you and your spouse must decide whether you want the IRS to contribute $3.00 of your tax money to a special fund to help pay for presidential election costs.

This will not increase your tax owed or decrease the amount of your refund. The money the IRS contributes to this fund is money that you have already paid.

- Mark an X in the first Yes box if you do want the IRS to contribute $3.00 to the special fund. Or mark an X in the first No box if you do not want the IRS to contribute $3.00 to the special fund.
- Mark an X in the second Yes box if your spouse does want the IRS to contribute $3.00 to the special fund. Or mark an X in the second No box if your spouse does not want the IRS to contribute $3.00 to the special fund.

SECTION 2: FILING STATUS

In this section of the 1040A, you must indicate your filing status. As discussed in Chapter 4, there are five types of filing status:

1. Single.
2. Married filing joint return.
3. Married filing separate return.
4. Head of household.
5. Qualifying widow(er) with dependent child.

Filing status	**1**	☐ Single
	2	☐ Married filing joint return (even if only one had income)
	3	☐ Married filing separate return. Enter spouse's social security number above and full name here. ▶ ________
Check only one box.	**4**	☐ Head of household (with qualifying person). (See page 20.) If the qualifying person is a child but not your dependent, enter this child's name here. ▶ ________
	5	☐ Qualifying widow(er) with dependent child (year spouse died ▶ 19). (See page 21.)

- Mark an X in the appropriate box.

  If you marked an X in box 3, print your spouse's full name in the space provided. Enter your spouse's Social Security number in the space provided at the top of the form.

  If you marked an X in box 4 and the qualifying person is a child who is not your dependent, print the child's name in the space provided.

  If you marked an X in box 5, print the year your spouse died in the space provided.

SECTION 3: YOUR EXEMPTIONS

In this section of the 1040A where you figure your exemptions, you must print personal information about yourself and your dependents.

Exemptions

6a ☐ **Yourself.** If your parent (or someone else) can claim you as a dependent on his or her tax return, **do not** check box 6a.

b ☐ **Spouse**

No. of boxes checked on 6a and 6b ____

c Dependents:

(1) First name Last name	(2) Dependent's social security number	(3) Dependent's relationship to you	(4) ✓ if qualifying child for child tax credit (see page 22)
			☐
			☐
			☐
			☐
			☐
			☐
			☐

If more than seven dependents, see page 21.

No. of your children on 6c who:
- **lived with you** ____
- **did not live with you due to divorce or separation (see page 23)** ____

Dependents on 6c not entered above ____

d Total number of exemptions claimed.

Add numbers entered on lines above ☐

6a. If you were not claimed as a dependent on someone else's income tax return, mark an X in box 6a.

6b. If you were married and are filing jointly, mark an X in box 6b.

6c. On the lines under box 6c, print:

- First and last (family) names of all your dependents (column 1).
- Social Security number of each dependent (column 2).
- The dependent's relationship to you (column 3).
- An X in the box, if the dependent is under age 17 AND is your son, daughter, adopted child, grandchild, stepchild, or foster child AND is a U.S. citizen (column 4).
- Look at the lines on the right side of the form in this section.

  On the top line, print the total number of boxes marked in 6a and 6b (0, 1, or 2).

  On the next line, to the right of 6c, print the number of your children who lived with you.
- On the next line, print the number of your children who did not live with you because of divorce or separation.
- On the next line, print the number of other dependents listed in 6c.
- Add the number of exemptions claimed in 6a, 6b, and 6c.

6d. Print the total in the box to the right of 6d.

SECTION 4: FIGURING TOTAL INCOME

In this section of the 1040A, you must print financial information about your income. This information includes:

- Total wages, salaries, and tips.
- Total taxable interest income.
- Total IRA and pension income.
- Unemployment compensation income.
- Social Security income.

Most people have only a few types of income.

Example

If you are a young working person, you probably do not receive Social Security income. When the form asks how much you receive in Social Security benefits, you would simply write a 0 (zero).

Income					
	7	Wages, salaries, tips, etc. Attach Form(s) W-2.		7	
Attach Copy B of your Forms W-2 and 1099-R here.	8a	**Taxable** interest. Attach Schedule 1 if required.		8a	
	b	**Tax-exempt** interest. DO NOT include on line 8a.	8b		
	9	Ordinary dividends. Attach Schedule 1 if required.		9	
If you did not get a W-2, see page 24.	10a	Total IRA distributions. 10a	**10b** Taxable amount (see page 24).	10b	
	11a	Total pensions and annuities. 11a	**11b** Taxable amount (see page 25).	11b	
Enclose, but do not staple, any payment.	12	Unemployment compensation.		12	
	13a	Social security benefits. 13a	**13b** Taxable amount (see page 27).	13b	
	14	Add lines 7 through 13b (far right column). This is your **total income.** ►		14	

7. Add up total wages, salaries, and tips. Print the total on line 7.
8. Add up the total taxable interest.
   - In 8a, print the total. (If the total exceeds $400, you must also complete Schedule 1. See the Appendix.)
   - Add up the total tax-exempt interest. In 8b, print the total.
9. Add up ordinary dividends. Print the total in the space on line 9. (If the total exceeds $400, you must also complete Schedule 1. See the Appendix.)

10a. Add up the total IRA income. In 10a, print the total.

10b. Add up the total taxable IRA income. In 10b, print the total.

11a. Add up the total pension income. In 11a, print the total.

11b. Add up the total taxable pension income. In 11b, print the total.

12. Add up the total unemployment compensation income. On line 12, print the total.

13a. Add up the total Social Security income. In 13a, print the total.

13b. Add up the total taxable Social Security income. In 13b, print the total.

14. Add the amounts on lines 7, 8a, 9, 10b, 11b, 12, and 13b. Print the total on line 14.

This amount is your **total income**.

SECTION 5: ADJUSTED GROSS INCOME

In this section, you calculate your adjusted gross income. If you have an IRA, you must first total the amount of IRA deduction that will reduce your taxable income.

If you do not have an IRA, skip to line 16.

Adjusted gross income			
	15	IRA deduction (see page 28).	15
	16	Student loan interest deduction (see page 28).	16
	17	Add lines 15 and 16. These are your **total adjustments.**	17
	18	Subtract line 17 from line 14. This is your **adjusted gross income.** If under $30,095 (under $10,030 if a child did not live with you), see the EIC instructions on page 36. ▶	18

For Disclosure, Privacy Act, and Paperwork Reduction Act Notice, see page 49. Cat. No. 11327A **1998 Form 1040A**

15. Add up your total IRA deduction. Print the total in space 15.
16. You may be eligible for a student loan interest deduction. If you paid interest on a student loan during the past year, refer to the instructions provided with the 1040A to see if you qualified and to fill out the student loan interest deduction worksheet.

    If you qualified, print the amount from the worksheet on line 16.

    If you did not qualify, print 0 on line 16.
17. Add the amounts on lines 15 and 16. Print the result on line 17. These are **total adjustments.**
18. Subtract the amount on line 17 from line 14 (line 14 – line 17). Print the result on line 18.
    - This is your **adjusted gross income**.
    - If this amount is less than $30,095, you should see the information on earned income credit (EIC) in the Appendix of this book. You may be able to pay less tax.

SECTION 6: FIGURING DEDUCTIONS

In this section of the 1040A, you must total the amount of deductions and subtract that amount from your total income.

1998 Form 1040A page 2

Taxable income			
	19	Enter the amount from line 18.	19
	20a	Check if: ☐ **You** were 65 or older ☐ Blind; ☐ **Spouse** was 65 or older ☐ Blind } **Enter number of boxes checked** ▶	20a ☐
	b	If you are married filing separately and your spouse itemizes deductions, see page 30 and check here . . . . . . ▶	20b ☐
	21	Enter the **standard deduction** for your filing status. **But** see page 31 if you checked any box on line 20a or 20b **OR** if someone can claim you as a dependent. • Single—$4,250 • Married filing jointly or Qualifying widow(er)—$7,100 • Head of household—$6,250 • Married filing separately—$3,550	21
	22	Subtract line 21 from line 19. If line 21 is more than line 19, enter -0-.	22
	23	Multiply $2,700 by the total number of exemptions claimed on line 6d.	23
	24	Subtract line 23 from line 22. If line 23 is more than line 22, enter -0-. This is your **taxable income.** ▶	24

19. Print the amount from line 18 on line 19.

20a. Mark an X in the small boxes if:

- You are 65 or older.
- Your spouse is 65 or older.
- You are blind.
- Your spouse is blind.

Count the number of boxes marked with an X. Print the total in the big box to the right of 20a.

20b. If you are married filing separately, AND your spouse files Form 1040, AND your spouse itemizes, mark an X in box 20b.

21. Enter the correct amount of the standard deduction for your filing status. The amounts are shown on the form.

- If you check any boxes in 20, or if someone can claim you as a dependent on his or her income tax, be sure to follow the special instructions.

22. Subtract the amount in 21 from the amount in 19 (line 19 – line 21) and print the result on line 22.

If the amount on line 21 is more than the amount on line 19, print 0 on line 22.

23. Multiply $2,700 times the amount on line 6d ($2,700 × line 6d) and print the result on line 23.

24. Subtract the amount on line 23 from the amount on line 22 (line 22 – line 23) and print the result on line 24.

- If the amount on line 23 is more than the amount on line 22, print 0 on line 24.
- The amount on line 24 is your taxable income.

SECTION 7: TAX, CREDITS, PAYMENTS

In this section, you must look up your tax in the tax tables and total the amount of your credits. These credits include:

- Credits for child-care expenses.
- Federal income tax withheld from your paychecks.
- Earned income credit for low-income taxpayers.

Tax, credits, and payments					
	25	Find the tax on the amount on line 24 (see page 31).			25
	26	Credit for child and dependent care expenses. Attach Schedule 2.	26		
	27	Credit for the elderly or the disabled. Attach Schedule 3.	27		
	28	Child tax credit (see page 32).	28		
	29	Education credits. Attach Form 8863.	29		
	30	Adoption credit. Attach Form 8839.	30		
	31	Add lines 26 through 30. These are your **total credits.**			31
	32	Subtract line 31 from line 25. If line 31 is more than line 25, enter -0-.			32
	33	Advance earned income credit payments from Form(s) W-2.			33
	34	Add lines 32 and 33. This is your **total tax.**		▶	34
	35	Total Federal income tax withheld from Forms W-2 and 1099.	35		
	36	1998 estimated tax payments and amount applied from 1997 return.	36		
	37a	**Earned income credit.** Attach Schedule EIC if you have a qualifying child.	37a		
	b	Nontaxable earned income: amount ▶ and type ▶			
	38	Additional child tax credit. Attach Form 8812.	38		
	39	Add lines 35, 36, 37a, and 38. These are your **total payments.**		▶	39

25. Look in the tax tables. Find your taxable income (line 24). Print the amount of tax on line 25.

26. If you had child-care expenses, you must include the form Schedule 2 with your 1040A. (See the Appendix for instructions.)

    - On line 26, write the amount of credit for child-care expenses from Schedule 2, line 9. If you had no child-care expenses, print 0 on line 26.

27. If you were an elderly or disabled person, you must include the form Schedule 3 with your 1040A.

    - On line 27, write the amount of this credit from Schedule 3. If you had no elderly or disabled person credit, print 0 on line 27.

28. If you did not have a qualifying child, print 0 on line 28 and continue to line 29.

    If you had a child who qualified for a tax credit, you will need to fill out the Child Tax Credit Worksheet. See the . This worksheet should not be submitted with the 1040A, but it should be kept for your own records.

    - On line 28, write the amount of the Child Tax Credit from line 11 of the Child Tax Credit Worksheet.

Child Tax Credit Worksheet–Line 28

▶ Keep for your records.

Do Not File

1. $400.00 ______________ . Multiply and enter the result . . . . 1. ________
Enter number of qualifying children (see page 32)

2. Enter the amount from Form 1040A, line 19 . . . . . 2. ________

3. Is line 2 above more than $55,000?

☐ **No.** Skip lines 3 through 5, enter -0- on line 6, and go to line 7.

☐ **Yes.** Enter: $75,000 if single, head of household, or qualifying widow(er); $110,000 if married filing jointly; $55,000 if married filing separately . . . . . 3. ________

4. Subtract line 3 from line 2. If zero or less, enter -0- here and on line 6, and go to line 7 . . . . 4. ________

5. Divide line 4 by $1,000. If the result is not a whole number, round it up to the next higher whole number (for example, round 0.01 to 1) . . . . 5. ________

6. Multiply $50 by the number on line 5 . . . . 6. ________

7. Subtract line 6 from line 1. If zero or less, **stop here;** you **cannot** take this credit . 7. ________

8. Enter the amount from Form 1040A, line 25 . . . . . 8. ________

9. Is line 1 above more than $800?

☐ **No.** Add the amounts from Form 1040A, lines 26, 27, and 29. Enter the total.

☐ **Yes.** Enter the amount from the worksheet on page 34. } 9. ________

10. Subtract line 9 above from line 8 . . . . 10. ________

11. **Child tax credit.** Enter the **smaller** of line 7 or line 10 here and on Form 1040A, line 28 ▶ 11. ________

TIP *If line 1 above is more than $800, you may be able to take the* ***Additional Child Tax Credit.*** *See page 32.*

1. In part 1, write the number of qualifying children you have. Multiply this number by 400 and write the answer on line 1.
2. On line 2, enter the amount from line 19 of Form 1040A.
3. If line 2 if less than $55,000 check No and skip lines 3 through 5. Write 0 on line 6 and continue on to line 7

   If line 2 is greater than $55,000 check Yes and enter the appropriate amount on line 3.
4. Subtract line 3 from line 2 (line 3 – line 2). If line 2 is larger than line 3, write 0 on lines 4 and 5 and go to line 7.
5. Divide line 4 by $1,000. If the answer is not a whole number, round it up to the next whole number. Write the answer on line 5.

6. Multiply line 5 by $50 and write the product on line 6.
7. Subtract line 6 from line 1 (line 1 – line 6). If line 6 is greater than line 1, STOP—you cannot take this credit. If line 1 is greater than line 6, write the remainder on line 7.
8. Write the amount from line 25 of Form 1040A.
9. If line 1 is greater than $800, check Yes. You will need to fill out another worksheet, which can be found in the instructions for the 1040A. If line 1 is less than $800, check No. Add the amounts from lines 26, 27, and 29 on Form 1040A. Write the sum on line 9.
10. Subtract line 9 from line 8 (line 9 – line 8). Write the remainder on line 10.
11. Look at line 7 and line 10. Write the smaller number on line 11 and on Form 1040A, line 28.

---

29. If you had post-secondary education expenses, you may qualify for education credits. Include Form 8863 with your return.
    - On line 29, write the amount of this credit from Form 8863. If you were not eligible for education credits, print 0 on line 29.
30. If you had adoption expenses, you must include Form 8839 with your 1040A.
    - On line 30, write the amount of this credit from Form 8839. If you had no adoption expenses, print 0 on line 30.
31. Add the figures from lines 26 through 30. Print the total on line 31.
    - These are your **total credits.**
32. Subtract the amount on line 31 from the amount on line 25 (line 25 – line 31) and print the result on line 32.
    - If line 31 is more than line 25, print 0 (zero) on line 32.
33. Add the amounts from box 9 on each of your W-2 forms. Print the total on line 33.
34. Add the amounts on lines 32 and 33. Print the total on line 34.
    - This amount is your **total tax.**
35. Add the amounts from box 2 on each of your W-2 forms and print the total on line 35.
36. If you sent estimated tax payments (for example, if you were self-employed), add the total of these payments and print the amount on line 36. If you had no estimated tax payments, print 0 on line 36.

37a. If you earned less than $30,095 AND line 18 on the 1040A form is less than $30,095 AND you are not "married filing separate return" on the 1040A form, you may be eligible to receive an earned income credit. If you have at least one dependent child, you must complete the Schedule EIC form (see the Appendix) and print the amount from the Earned Income Credit worksheet on line 37a. Otherwise, print 0 on line 37a.

37b. Certain types of income are not taxable, but you must include them on your tax return to see if you can receive the earned income credit. Examples of nontaxable earned income are housing allowances or meals and lodging provided by your employer or the military.

If you received nontaxable earned income from your employer, write the amount and type on line 37b.

NOTE: Welfare, SSI, and Food Stamps are not earned income. Do not include them in 37b.

---

38. If you qualified for a Child Tax Credit you may be eligible for an additional child tax credit. It is necessary to fill out Form 8812 (not included in this book) to calculate the credit. Write this amount on line 38. If you do not qualify write 0 on line 38.

39. Add the amounts on lines 35, 36, 37a, and 38. Print the total on line 39.
    - This is your **total tax payment.**

SECTION 8: REFUND OR TAXES OWED

In this section of the 1040A, you must compare the amount of tax credits and payments with the amount of taxes owed. This will determine whether you receive a refund or if you must pay more taxes.

Refund	**40**	If line 39 is more than line 34, subtract line 34 from line 39. This is the amount you **overpaid.**	40	
Have it directly deposited! See page 43 and fill in 41b, 41c, and 41d.	**41a**	Amount of line 40 you want **refunded to you.**	41a	
	b	Routing number ☐☐☐☐☐☐☐☐☐ **c** Type: ☐ Checking ☐ Savings		
	d	Account number ☐☐☐☐☐☐☐☐☐☐☐☐☐☐☐☐☐		
	42	Amount of line 40 you want **applied to your 1999 estimated tax.** 42		

40. Look to see if the amount on line 39 is larger than the amount on line 34. If it is smaller, go to line 43. If it is larger, subtract the amount on line 34 from the amount on line 39 (line 34 – line 39). Print the result on line 40.
    - You have paid too much in taxes and can receive a refund for this amount.

41a. Print the number from line 40 on line 41a if you want the money refunded to you. (Most people prefer this.)

The IRS will now directly deposit your refund in the bank if you have a checking or savings account. This is a good idea because it prevents lost or stolen income tax refund checks. If you prefer to receive a refund check, leave 41b, 41c, and 41d blank.

41b. Print the routing number of your bank. (Ask the bank for this nine-digit number.)

41c. Put an X in the correct box to indicate whether your income tax refund is to be deposited into your checking or savings account.

41d. Write your account number in the boxes.

42. You can have all or part of your refund applied to the next year's taxes. If you prefer to receive the refund, print 0 on line 42.

43. If the amount on line 39 is smaller than the amount on line 34, subtract the amount on line 39 from the amount on line 34 (line 34 – line 39). Print the result on line 43.

    - You owe this amount of taxes to the IRS.
    - Prepare a check or money order, payable to the IRS, for this amount.
    - Print your name, address, Social Security number, daytime telephone number, and "199_ Form 1040A" on the check or money order.

44. Write a 0 on line 44 unless you owe a penalty. Refer to the instructions on the form regarding penalties.

SECTION 9: SIGNING YOUR RETURN

In this final section of the 1040A, you (and your spouse) must sign and date your income tax report. You must also indicate your occupation(s).

Sign here	Under penalties of perjury, I declare that I have examined this return and accompanying schedules and statements, and to the best of my knowledge and belief, they are true, correct, and accurately list all amounts and sources of income I received during the tax year. Declaration of preparer (other than the taxpayer) is based on all information of which the preparer has any knowledge.			
Joint return? See page 19.	Your signature	Date	Your occupation	Daytime telephone number (optional)
Keep a copy for your records.	Spouse's signature. If joint return, BOTH must sign.	Date	Spouse's occupation	( )
Paid preparer's use only	Preparer's signature	Date	Check if self-employed ☐	Preparer's social security no.
	Firm's name (or yours if self-employed) and address			EIN
				ZIP code

- In the area that says "Your signature," sign your name.
- In the area that says "Spouse's signature" (if a joint return, both must sign), have your spouse sign, if applicable.
- Print the date beside each signature.
- Print the occupation beside each date.

Paid preparer

- If you paid a person to prepare your taxes, that person must fill in this section. Otherwise, leave it blank.

1040A FINAL PROCEDURES

- Make a copy of this form for your records.
- Staple Copy B of your W-2 form(s) to the original 1040A form.
- If you owe taxes, staple your check or money order, on top of the W-2 form(s), to the original 1040A form.
- Send Copy B of the W-2 forms and the original 1040A, plus any payment, to your Internal Revenue Service Center. Select the address from the list below.

Alabama—Memphis, TN 37501
Alaska—Ogden, UT 84201
Arizona—Ogden, UT 84201
Arkansas—Memphis, TN 37501
California—*Counties of Alpine, Amador, Butts, Calaveras, Colusa, Contra Costa, Del Norte, El Dorado, Glenn, Humboldt, Lake, Lassen, Marin, Mendocino, Modoc, Napa, Nevada, Placer, Plumas, Sacramento, San Joaquin, Shasta, Sierra, Siskiyou, Solano, Sonoma, Sutter, Tehama, Trinity, Yolo, and Yuba*—Ogden, UT 84201
All other counties—Fresno, CA 93888
Colorado—Ogden, UT 84201
Connecticut—Andover, MA 05501
Delaware—Philadelphia, PA 19255
District of Columbia—Philadelphia, PA 19255
Florida—Atlanta, GA 39901
Georgia—Atlanta, GA 39901
Hawaii—Fresno, CA 93888
Idaho—Ogden, UT 84201
Illinois—Kansas City, MO 64999
Indiana—Cincinnati, OH 45999
Iowa—Kansas City, MO 64999
Kansas—Austin, TX 73301
Kentucky—Cincinnati, OH 45999
Louisiana—Memphis, TN 37501
Maine—Andover, MA 05501
Maryland—Philadelphia, PA 19255
Massachusetts—Andover, MA 05501
Michigan—Cincinnati, OH 45999
Minnesota—Kansas City, MO 64999
Mississippi—Memphis, TN 37501
Missouri—Kansas City, MO 64999
Montana—Ogden, UT 84201
Nebraska—Ogden, UT 84201
Nevada—Ogden, UT 84201
New Hampshire—Andover, MA 05501
New Jersey—Holtsville, NY 00501
New Mexico—Austin, TX 73301
New York—*New York City and counties of Nassau, Rockland, Suffolk, and Westchester*—Holtsville, NY 00501
All other counties—Andover, MA 05501
North Carolina—Memphis, TN 37501
North Dakota—Ogden, UT 84201
Ohio—Cincinnati, OH 45999
Oklahoma—Austin, TX 73301
Oregon—Ogden, UT 84201
Pennsylvania—Philadelphia, PA 19255
Rhode Island—Andover, MA 05501
South Carolina—Atlanta, GA 39901
South Dakota—Ogden, UT 84201
Tennessee—Memphis, TN 37501
Texas—Austin, TX 73301
Utah—Ogden, UT 84201
Vermont—Andover, MA 05501
Virginia—Philadelphia, PA 19255
Washington—Ogden, UT 84201
West Virginia—Cincinnati, OH 45999
Wisconsin—Kansas City, MO 64999
Wyoming—Ogden, UT 84201
American Samoa—Philadelphia, PA 19255
Guam—Commissioner of Revenue and Taxation
855 West Marine Dr.
Agana, GU 96910
Puerto Rico *(or if excluding income under section 933)*—Philadelphia, PA 19255
Virgin Islands: Nonpermanent residents—
Philadelphia, PA 19255
Virgin Islands: Permanent residents—
V.I. Bureau of Internal Revenue
Lockharts Garden No. 1A
Charlotte Amalie
St. Thomas, VI 00802
Foreign country: *U.S. citizens and those filing Form 2555, Form 2555-EZ, or Form 4563*—
Philadelphia, PA 19255
All A.P.O. and F.P.O. addresses—
Philadelphia, PA 19255

YOUR 1040A

If you wish to complete a 1040A form for yourself, you should be aware that the forms and amounts in this book may not be accurate for the current year.

You may fill out the forms in this book for practice, but you should use a current form and use the amounts on that form when you prepare your taxes.

Information on where to get help is in Chapter 8.

COMPLETING THE 1040A—EXERCISE 2

ACTIVITY: Fill out the form for Mary Wong's family.

Mary Wong is a bookkeeper. Her husband died four years ago, and she has not remarried. Her son, Daniel, is six years old.

She earned $27,692 in 1998. Her savings account at the bank earned $100 in interest.

Her deductions total $3,000. She had $3,094 withheld from her year's earnings.

Their Social Security numbers are:

Mary: 987-33-1234

Daniel: 777-32-4503

They live at 12 Mountain Drive, Apt. 7D, Stoneplain, NY 10000. She wants to contribute to the Presidential Election Campaign fund.

1040A FOR MARY WONG—PAGE 1

Form **1040A** Department of the Treasury–Internal Revenue Service
U.S. Individual Income Tax Return **1998** IRS Use Only–Do not write or staple in this space.
OMB No. 1545-0085

Label (See page 18.)
Use the IRS label. Otherwise, please print or type.
LABEL HERE

Your first name and initial	Last name		**Your social security number**
If a joint return, spouse's first name and initial	Last name		**Spouse's social security number**
Home address (number and street). If you have a P.O. box, see page 19.		Apt. no.	
City, town or post office, state, and ZIP code. If you have a foreign address, see page 19.			

▲ IMPORTANT! ▲ You **must** enter your SSN(s) above.

Presidential Election Campaign Fund (See page 19.) | Yes | No
Do you want $3 to go to this fund? . . . .
If a joint return, does your spouse want $3 to go to this fund?

Note: *Checking "Yes" will not change your tax or reduce your refund.*

Filing status
Check only one box.

1 ☐ Single
2 ☐ Married filing joint return (even if only one had income)
3 ☐ Married filing separate return. Enter spouse's social security number above and full name here. ▶
4 ☐ Head of household (with qualifying person). (See page 20.) If the qualifying person is a child but not your dependent, enter this child's name here. ▶
5 ☐ Qualifying widow(er) with dependent child (year spouse died ▶ 19). (See page 21.)

Exemptions

6a ☐ **Yourself.** If your parent (or someone else) can claim you as a dependent on his or her tax return, **do not** check box 6a.
b ☐ **Spouse**

No. of boxes checked on 6a and 6b ____

c **Dependents:**

If more than seven dependents, see page 21.

(1) First name Last name	(2) Dependent's social security number	(3) Dependent's relationship to you	(4) ✓ if qualified child for child tax credit (see page 22)
			☐
			☐
			☐
			☐
			☐
			☐
			☐

No. of your children on 6c who:
• **lived with you** ____
• **did not live with you due to divorce or separation (see page 23)** ____
Dependents on 6c not entered above ____
Add numbers entered on lines above ☐

d Total number of exemptions claimed.

Income

Attach Copy B of your Forms W-2 and 1099-R here.

If you did not get a W-2, see page 24.

Enclose, but do not staple, any payment.

Line	Description			Line	Amount
7	Wages, salaries, tips, etc. Attach Form(s) W-2.			7	
8a	**Taxable** interest. Attach Schedule 1 if required.			8a	
b	**Tax-exempt** interest. DO NOT include on line 8a.	8b			
9	Ordinary dividends. Attach Schedule 1 if required.			9	
10a	Total IRA distributions.	10a	**10b** Taxable amount (see page 24).	10b	
11a	Total pensions and annuities.	11a	**11b** Taxable amount (see page 25).	11b	
12	Unemployment compensation.			12	
13a	Social security benefits.	13a	**13b** Taxable amount (see page 27).	13b	
14	Add lines 7 through 13b (far right column). This is your **total income.**			▶ 14	

Adjusted gross income

Line	Description			Line	Amount
15	IRA deduction (see page 28).	15			
16	Student loan interest deduction (see page 28).	16			
17	Add lines 15 and 16. These are your **total adjustments.**			17	
18	Subtract line 17 from line 14. This is your **adjusted gross income.** If under $30,095 (under $10,030 if a child did not live with you), see the EIC instructions on page 36.			▶ 18	

For Disclosure, Privacy Act, and Paperwork Reduction Act Notice, see page 49. Cat. No. 11327A **1998 Form 1040A**

1040A FOR MARY WONG—PAGE 2

1998 Form 1040A page 2

Taxable income

19 Enter the amount from line 18. 19

20a Check if: ☐ **You** were 65 or older ☐ Blind ☐ **Spouse** was 65 or older ☐ Blind **Enter number of boxes checked** ▶ 20a ☐

b If you are married filing separately and your spouse itemizes deductions, see page 30 and check here . . . . . . ▶ 20b ☐

21 Enter the **standard deduction** for your filing status. **But** see page 31 if you checked any box on line 20a or 20b **OR** if someone can claim you as a dependent.
- Single–$4,250 • Married filing jointly or Qualifying widow(er)–$7,100
- Head of household–$6,250 • Married filing separately–$3,550 21

22 Subtract line 21 from line 19. If line 21 is more than line 19, enter -0-. 22

23 Multiply $2,700 by the total number of exemptions claimed on line 6d. 23

24 Subtract line 23 from line 22. If line 23 is more than line 22, enter -0-. This is your **taxable income.** ▶ 24

Tax, credits, and payments

25 Find the tax on the amount on line 24 (see page 31). 25

26 Credit for child and dependent care expenses. Attach Schedule 2. 26

27 Credit for the elderly or the disabled. Attach Schedule 3. 27

28 Child tax credit (see page 32). 28

29 Education credits. Attach Form 8863. 29

30 Adoption credit. Attach Form 8839. 30

31 Add lines 26 through 30. These are your **total credits.** 31

32 Subtract line 31 from line 25. If line 31 is more than line 25, enter -0-. 32

33 Advance earned income credit payments from Form(s) W-2. 33

34 Add lines 32 and 33. This is your **total tax.** ▶ 34

35 Total Federal income tax withheld from Forms W-2 and 1099. 35

36 1998 estimated tax payments and amount applied from 1997 return. 36

37a **Earned income credit.** Attach Schedule EIC if you have a qualifying child. 37a

b Nontaxable earned income: amount ▶ and type ▶

38 Additional child tax credit. Attach Form 8812. 38

39 Add lines 35, 36, 37a, and 38. These are your **total payments.** ▶ 39

Refund

Have it directly deposited! See page 43 and fill in 41b, 41c, and 41d.

40 If line 39 is more than line 34, subtract line 34 from line 39. This is the amount you **overpaid.** 40

41a Amount of line 40 you want **refunded to you.** 41a

b Routing number ☐☐☐☐☐☐☐☐☐ **c** Type: ☐ Checking ☐ Savings

d Account number ☐☐☐☐☐☐☐☐☐☐☐☐☐☐☐☐☐

42 Amount of line 40 you want **applied to your 1999 estimated tax** 42

Amount you owe

43 If line 34 is more than line 39, subtract line 39 from line 34. This is the **amount you owe.** For details on how to pay, see page 44. 43

44 Estimated tax penalty (see page 44). 44

Sign here

Joint return? See page 19.
Keep a copy for your records.

Under penalties of perjury, I declare that I have examined this return and accompanying schedules and statements, and to the best of my knowledge and belief, they are true, correct, and accurately list all amounts and sources of income I received during the tax year. Declaration of preparer (other than the taxpayer) is based on all information of which the preparer has any knowledge.

Your signature	Date	Your occupation	Daytime telephone number (optional)
Spouse's signature. If joint return, BOTH must sign.	Date	Spouse's occupation	( )

Paid preparer's use only

Preparer's signature	Date	Check if self-employed ☐	Preparer's social security no.
Firm's name (or yours if self-employed) and address			EIN
			ZIP code

1040A FOR MARY WONG—CHILD TAX CREDIT WORKSHEET

Do Not File

Child Tax Credit Worksheet–Line 28

▶ Keep for your records.

1. $400.00 ________ . Multiply and enter the result . . . . 1. ________

Enter number of qualifying children (see page 32)

2. Enter the amount from Form 1040A, line 19 . . . . . . 2. ________

3. Is line 2 above more than $55,000?

☐ **No.** Skip lines 3 through 5, enter -0- on line 6, and go to line 7.

☐ **Yes.** Enter: $75,000 if single, head of household, or qualifying widow(er); $110,000 if married filing jointly; $55,000 if married filing separately . . . . . . 3. ________

4. Subtract line 3 from line 2. If zero or less, enter -0- here and on line 6, and go to line 7 . . . . 4. ________

5. Divide line 4 by $1,000. If the result is not a whole number, round it up to the next higher whole number (for example, round 0.01 to 1) . . . . 5. ________

6. Multiply $50 by the number on line 5 . . . . 6. ________

7. Subtract line 6 from line 1. If zero or less, **stop here;** you **cannot** take this credit . 7. ________

8. Enter the amount from Form 1040A, line 25 . . . . . . 8. ________

9. Is line 1 above more than $800?

☐ **No.** Add the amounts from Form 1040A, lines 26, 27, and 29. Enter the total.

☐ **Yes.** Enter the amount from the worksheet on page 34.

} 9. ________

10. Subtract line 9 above from line 8 . . . . 10. ________

11. **Child tax credit.** Enter the **smaller** of line 7 or line 10 here and on Form 1040A, line 28 ▶ 11. ________

TIP *If line 1 above is more than $800, you may be able to take the* ***Additional Child Tax Credit.*** *See page 32.*

COMPLETING THE 1040A—EXERCISE 3

Activity: Fill out the form for Ramon Flores.

Ramon Flores is a dishwasher and a part-time janitor. He is not married but supports his two younger sisters with his salary. They do not live with him in the United States, but live in Guadalajara, Mexico.

He earned $11,600 from his first job and $5,500 from his second job. He has no savings account, and his deductions total $400. His employers withheld $1,200 from his pay.

Ramon has requested ITI numbers (by completing W-7 forms for each of his sisters) so that they may be included on his income tax return. Their numbers are:

Silvia Flores: 800-31-9906

Irma Flores: 800-92-7527

Ramon's Social Security number is 224-27-8103. He lives at 7184 Washington Avenue, Apt. C, Flint, Michigan 40000. He wants to contribute to the Presidential Election Campaign fund.

Questions

- Can Ramon use the 1040EZ instead of the 1040A?
- Can Ramon file as head of household?
- Is Ramon eligible for the earned income credit? (See the Appendix.)

1040A FOR RAMON FLORES—PAGE 1

Form **1040A** Department of the Treasury–Internal Revenue Service
U.S. Individual Income Tax Return **1998** IRS Use Only–Do not write or staple in this space.

OMB No. 1545-0085

Label (See page 18.)

Use the IRS label. Otherwise, please print or type.

LABEL HERE

Your first name and initial	Last name		Your social security number
If a joint return, spouse's first name and initial	Last name		Spouse's social security number
Home address (number and street). If you have a P.O. box, see page 19.		Apt. no.	
City, town or post office, state, and ZIP code. If you have a foreign address, see page 19.			

▲ IMPORTANT! ▲ You **must** enter your SSN(s) above.

Presidential Election Campaign Fund (See page 19.)

	Yes	No
Do you want $3 to go to this fund?		
If a joint return, does your spouse want $3 to go to this fund?		

Note: *Checking "Yes" will not change your tax or reduce your refund.*

Filing status

Check only one box.

1 ☐ Single
2 ☐ Married filing joint return (even if only one had income)
3 ☐ Married filing separate return. Enter spouse's social security number above and full name here. ▶
4 ☐ Head of household (with qualifying person). (See page 20.) If the qualifying person is a child but not your dependent, enter this child's name here. ▶
5 ☐ Qualifying widow(er) with dependent child (year spouse died ▶ 19). (See page 21.)

Exemptions

6a ☐ **Yourself.** If your parent (or someone else) can claim you as a dependent on his or her tax return, **do not** check box 6a.
b ☐ **Spouse**

No. of boxes checked on 6a and 6b

c **Dependents:**

If more than seven dependents, see page 21.

(1) First name Last name	(2) Dependent's social security number	(3) Dependent's relationship to you	(4)✓if qualified child for child tax credit (see page 22)
			☐
			☐
			☐
			☐
			☐
			☐
			☐

No. of your children on 6c who:
- **lived with you**
- **did not live with you due to divorce or separation (see page 23)**

Dependents on 6c not entered above

d Total number of exemptions claimed.

Add numbers entered on lines above

Income

Attach Copy B of your Forms W-2 and 1099-R here.

If you did not get a W-2, see page 24.

Enclose, but do not staple, any payment.

Line	Description			Box
7	Wages, salaries, tips, etc. Attach Form(s) W-2.			7
8a	**Taxable** interest. Attach Schedule 1 if required.			8a
b	**Tax-exempt** interest. DO NOT include on line 8a.	8b		
9	Ordinary dividends. Attach Schedule 1 if required.			9
10a	Total IRA distributions.	10a	**10b** Taxable amount (see page 24).	10b
11a	Total pensions and annuities.	11a	**11b** Taxable amount (see page 25).	11b
12	Unemployment compensation.			12
13a	Social security benefits.	13a	**13b** Taxable amount (see page 27).	13b
14	Add lines 7 through 13b (far right column). This is your **total income.**			▶ 14

Adjusted gross income

Line	Description		Box
15	IRA deduction (see page 28).	15	
16	Student loan interest deduction (see page 28).	16	
17	Add lines 15 and 16. These are your **total adjustments.**		17
18	Subtract line 17 from line 14. This is your **adjusted gross income.** If under $30,095 (under $10,030 if a child did not live with you), see the EIC instructions on page 36.		▶ 18

For Disclosure, Privacy Act, and Paperwork Reduction Act Notice, see page 49. Cat. No. 11327A **1998 Form 1040A**

1040A FOR RAMON FLORES—PAGE 2

1998 Form 1040A page 2

Taxable income

19 Enter the amount from line 18. 19

20a Check if: ☐ **You** were 65 or older ☐ Blind / ☐ **Spouse** was 65 or older ☐ Blind } **Enter number of boxes checked** ▶ 20a ☐

b If you are married filing separately and your spouse itemizes deductions, see page 30 and check here . . . . ▶ 20b ☐

21 Enter the **standard deduction** for your filing status. **But** see page 31 if you checked any box on line 20a or 20b **OR** if someone can claim you as a dependent.
- Single—$4,250
- Married filing jointly or Qualifying widow(er)—$7,100
- Head of household—$6,250
- Married filing separately—$3,550 21

22 Subtract line 21 from line 19. If line 21 is more than line 19, enter -0-. 22

23 Multiply $2,700 by the total number of exemptions claimed on line 6d. 23

24 Subtract line 23 from line 22. If line 23 is more than line 22, enter -0-. This is your **taxable income.** ▶ 24

Tax, credits, and payments

25 Find the tax on the amount on line 24 (see page 31). 25

26 Credit for child and dependent care expenses. Attach Schedule 2. 26

27 Credit for the elderly or the disabled. Attach Schedule 3. 27

28 Child tax credit (see page 32). 28

29 Education credits. Attach Form 8863. 29

30 Adoption credit. Attach Form 8839. 30

31 Add lines 26 through 30. These are your **total credits.** 31

32 Subtract line 31 from line 25. If line 31 is more than line 25, enter -0-. 32

33 Advance earned income credit payments from Form(s) W-2. 33

34 Add lines 32 and 33. This is your **total tax.** ▶ 34

35 Total Federal income tax withheld from Forms W-2 and 1099. 35

36 1998 estimated tax payments and amount applied from 1997 return. 36

37a **Earned income credit.** Attach Schedule EIC if you have a qualifying child. 37a

b Nontaxable earned income: amount ▶ and type ▶

38 Additional child tax credit. Attach Form 8812. 38

39 Add lines 35, 36, 37a, and 38. These are your **total payments.** ▶ 39

Refund

Have it directly deposited! See page 43 and fill in 41b, 41c, and 41d.

40 If line 39 is more than line 34, subtract line 34 from line 39. This is the amount you **overpaid.** 40

41a Amount of line 40 you want **refunded to you.** 41a

b Routing number ☐☐☐☐☐☐☐☐☐ **c** Type: ☐ Checking ☐ Savings

d Account number ☐☐☐☐☐☐☐☐☐☐☐☐☐☐☐☐☐

42 Amount of line 40 you want **applied to your 1999 estimated tax.** 42

Amount you owe

43 If line 34 is more than line 39, subtract line 39 from line 34. This is the **amount you owe.** For details on how to pay, see page 44. 43

44 Estimated tax penalty (see page 44). 44

Sign here

Joint return? See page 19. Keep a copy for your records.

Under penalties of perjury, I declare that I have examined this return and accompanying schedules and statements, and to the best of my knowledge and belief, they are true, correct, and accurately list all amounts and sources of income I received during the tax year. Declaration of preparer (other than the taxpayer) is based on all information of which the preparer has any knowledge.

Your signature	Date	Your occupation	Daytime telephone number (optional)
Spouse's signature. If joint return, BOTH must sign.	Date	Spouse's occupation	( )

Paid preparer's use only

Preparer's signature	Date	Check if self-employed ☐	Preparer's social security no.
Firm's name (or yours if self-employed) and address			EIN
			ZIP code

CHAPTER 8

Where to Get Help

This chapter tells you how to get tax help from:

- IRS
- Libraries
- Tax preparers
- Phone book

VOCABULARY

ACTIVITY: The definition for each of these words is in the Glossary. As a vocabulary exercise, you may try to write a definition for each word before you look up its meaning in the Glossary.

fee

assistor

attorney

accountant

HELP FROM THE IRS

The IRS provides many ways to help taxpayers prepare their income tax return forms.

- **Publication 17**

  A tax guide for individuals, full of information on how to prepare your return and how to get more information.

  The publication is free, and you can order it by telephone or by mail.

- **Other IRS publications**

  Many IRS publications are available that provide detailed information on special topics.

  Some publications are available in Spanish.

  Publications are free, and you can order them from the IRS distribution center for your region.

- **The Internet:** www.irs.ustreas.gov
- **Tele-Tax**

  Recorded tax information on about 150 topics.

  Look in your phone book for the "Internal Revenue Service" in the U.S. Government Offices section for the phone number for your area, or consult Publication 17. The service is free.
- **VITA (Volunteer Income Tax Assistance) and TCE (Tax Counseling for the Elderly)**

  Free help for older, disabled, and non-English-speaking people.

  Call the IRS in your area to request the service.
- **Free tax help from the IRS**

  Order Publication 910 for a list of free publications and services available.

  Assistors are available at many local IRS offices. They can help you prepare your own return in a group setting. Call your local office for information.

  You may telephone the IRS for answers to questions about your return.

  You can send written questions to your IRS district director.
- **Forms by mail**

  You can request forms by mail by calling the IRS Forms Distribution Center in your region.

  The forms are free.

LIBRARIES

- **Forms**

  Commonly used forms, such as the 1040EZ and 1040A, are available in most libraries starting in December and January.
- **Videotaped instructions**

  Some libraries have videotaped instructions on how to fill out the tax return form.
- **Books**

  Libraries often have books with information on how to file your income tax. However, you must remember that the procedures change every year. You can use the books for general information, but be sure to look at the forms and instructions for current information.

  You can purchase books with current information from many bookstores. They are usually available in December and January. Many of these books are good if you need help with the long form, 1040, and if you itemize deductions.

TAX PREPARERS

Several types of tax preparers will fill out your income tax return form for you for a fee. These include:

- **Accountants**

  Some, but not all, are CPAs.

- **Professional tax preparers**

  Some people specialize in filling out tax returns. They are not necessarily accountants, but they are specially trained to fill out tax forms. They often advertise beginning in December and January.

  Be sure to compare services and prices of different tax preparers.

- **Tax attorneys**

  Some lawyers specialize in taxes, but it is not usually necessary to have an attorney fill out a tax form.

- **Tax preparation software**

  If you have a computer and a printer, there are a number of software programs that can help you complete your tax form.

  The advantage of these programs is that they perform the calculations for you.

You must remember that you are responsible for paying interest and penalties if you or your tax preparer makes a mistake.

TAX HELP—PHONE BOOK

Look in your phone book for the phone numbers and addresses of the following organizations.

- IRS information is generally in the "U.S. Government Pages" of the phone book, at the beginning of the white pages, or under "U.S. Government" in the white or business pages.
- The library information is generally in the city or county "Government Pages" of the phone book, at the beginning of the white pages, or under the name of the city or county in the white or business pages.

	Organization	Phone Number	Address
IRS	Federal forms and publications		
	Office locations		
	Tele-tax		
Library			

Tax Tables

1998 Tax Table

For persons with taxable incomes of less than $50,000

Example. Mr. and Mrs. Green are filing a joint return. Their taxable income on line 24 of Form 1040A is $23,250. First, they find the $23,250–23,300 income line. Next, they find the column for married filing jointly and read down the column. The amount shown where the income line and filing status column meet is $3,491. This is the tax amount they should enter on line 25 of Form 1040A.

At least	But less than	Single	Married filing jointly *	Married filing sepa-rately	Head of a house-hold
		Your tax is—			
23,200	**23,250**	3,484	3,484	3,750	3,484
23,250	**23,300**	3,491	(3,491)	3,764	3,491
23,300	**23,350**	3,499	3,499	3,778	3,499
23,350	**23,400**	3,506	3,506	3,792	3,506

If Form 1040A, line 24, is—		And you are—			
At least	But less than	Single	Married filing jointly *	Married filing sepa-rately	Head of a house-hold
		Your tax is—			
$0	**$5**	$0	$0	$0	$0
5	**15**	2	2	2	2
15	**25**	3	3	3	3
25	**50**	6	6	6	6
50	**75**	9	9	9	9
75	**100**	13	13	13	13
100	**125**	17	17	17	17
125	**150**	21	21	21	21
150	**175**	24	24	24	24
175	**200**	28	28	28	28
200	**225**	32	32	32	32
225	**250**	36	36	36	36
250	**275**	39	39	39	39
275	**300**	43	43	43	43
300	**325**	47	47	47	47
325	**350**	51	51	51	51
350	**375**	54	54	54	54
375	**400**	58	58	58	58
400	**425**	62	62	62	62
425	**450**	66	66	66	66
450	**475**	69	69	69	69
475	**500**	73	73	73	73
500	**525**	77	77	77	77
525	**550**	81	81	81	81
550	**575**	84	84	84	84
575	**600**	88	88	88	88
600	**625**	92	92	92	92
625	**650**	96	96	96	96
650	**675**	99	99	99	99
675	**700**	103	103	103	103
700	**725**	107	107	107	107
725	**750**	111	111	111	111
750	**775**	114	114	114	114
775	**800**	118	118	118	118
800	**825**	122	122	122	122
825	**850**	126	126	126	126
850	**875**	129	129	129	129
875	**900**	133	133	133	133
900	**925**	137	137	137	137
925	**950**	141	141	141	141
950	**975**	144	144	144	144
975	**1,000**	148	148	148	148
1,000					
1,000	**1,025**	152	152	152	152
1,025	**1,050**	156	156	156	156
1,050	**1,075**	159	159	159	159
1,075	**1,100**	163	163	163	163
1,100	**1,125**	167	167	167	167
1,125	**1,150**	171	171	171	171
1,150	**1,175**	174	174	174	174
1,175	**1,200**	178	178	178	178
1,200	**1,225**	182	182	182	182
1,225	**1,250**	186	186	186	186
1,250	**1,275**	189	189	189	189
1,275	**1,300**	193	193	193	193

If Form 1040A, line 24, is—		And you are—			
At least	But less than	Single	Married filing jointly *	Married filing sepa-rately	Head of a house-hold
		Your tax is—			
1,300	**1,325**	197	197	197	197
1,325	**1,350**	201	201	201	201
1,350	**1,375**	204	204	204	204
1,375	**1,400**	208	208	208	208
1,400	**1,425**	212	212	212	212
1,425	**1,450**	216	216	216	216
1,450	**1,475**	219	219	219	219
1,475	**1,500**	223	223	223	223
1,500	**1,525**	227	227	227	227
1,525	**1,550**	231	231	231	231
1,550	**1,575**	234	234	234	234
1,575	**1,600**	238	238	238	238
1,600	**1,625**	242	242	242	242
1,625	**1,650**	246	246	246	246
1,650	**1,675**	249	249	249	249
1,675	**1,700**	253	253	253	253
1,700	**1,725**	257	257	257	257
1,725	**1,750**	261	261	261	261
1,750	**1,775**	264	264	264	264
1,775	**1,800**	268	268	268	268
1,800	**1,825**	272	272	272	272
1,825	**1,850**	276	276	276	276
1,850	**1,875**	279	279	279	279
1,875	**1,900**	283	283	283	283
1,900	**1,925**	287	287	287	287
1,925	**1,950**	291	291	291	291
1,950	**1,975**	294	294	294	294
1,975	**2,000**	298	298	298	298
2,000					
2,000	**2,025**	302	302	302	302
2,025	**2,050**	306	306	306	306
2,050	**2,075**	309	309	309	309
2,075	**2,100**	313	313	313	313
2,100	**2,125**	317	317	317	317
2,125	**2,150**	321	321	321	321
2,150	**2,175**	324	324	324	324
2,175	**2,200**	328	328	328	328
2,200	**2,225**	332	332	332	332
2,225	**2,250**	336	336	336	336
2,250	**2,275**	339	339	339	339
2,275	**2,300**	343	343	343	343
2,300	**2,325**	347	347	347	347
2,325	**2,350**	351	351	351	351
2,350	**2,375**	354	354	354	354
2,375	**2,400**	358	358	358	358
2,400	**2,425**	362	362	362	362
2,425	**2,450**	366	366	366	366
2,450	**2,475**	369	369	369	369
2,475	**2,500**	373	373	373	373
2,500	**2,525**	377	377	377	377
2,525	**2,550**	381	381	381	381
2,550	**2,575**	384	384	384	384
2,575	**2,600**	388	388	388	388
2,600	**2,625**	392	392	392	392
2,625	**2,650**	396	396	396	396
2,650	**2,675**	399	399	399	399
2,675	**2,700**	403	403	403	403

If Form 1040A, line 24, is—		And you are—			
At least	But less than	Single	Married filing jointly *	Married filing sepa-rately	Head of a house-hold
		Your tax is—			
2,700	**2,725**	407	407	407	407
2,725	**2,750**	411	411	411	411
2,750	**2,775**	414	414	414	414
2,775	**2,800**	418	418	418	418
2,800	**2,825**	422	422	422	422
2,825	**2,850**	426	426	426	426
2,850	**2,875**	429	429	429	429
2,875	**2,900**	433	433	433	433
2,900	**2,925**	437	437	437	437
2,925	**2,950**	441	441	441	441
2,950	**2,975**	444	444	444	444
2,975	**3,000**	448	448	448	448
3,000					
3,000	**3,050**	454	454	454	454
3,050	**3,100**	461	461	461	461
3,100	**3,150**	469	469	469	469
3,150	**3,200**	476	476	476	476
3,200	**3,250**	484	484	484	484
3,250	**3,300**	491	491	491	491
3,300	**3,350**	499	499	499	499
3,350	**3,400**	506	506	506	506
3,400	**3,450**	514	514	514	514
3,450	**3,500**	521	521	521	521
3,500	**3,550**	529	529	529	529
3,550	**3,600**	536	536	536	536
3,600	**3,650**	544	544	544	544
3,650	**3,700**	551	551	551	551
3,700	**3,750**	559	559	559	559
3,750	**3,800**	566	566	566	566
3,800	**3,850**	574	574	574	574
3,850	**3,900**	581	581	581	581
3,900	**3,950**	589	589	589	589
3,950	**4,000**	596	596	596	596
4,000					
4,000	**4,050**	604	604	604	604
4,050	**4,100**	611	611	611	611
4,100	**4,150**	619	619	619	619
4,150	**4,200**	626	626	626	626
4,200	**4,250**	634	634	634	634
4,250	**4,300**	641	641	641	641
4,300	**4,350**	649	649	649	649
4,350	**4,400**	656	656	656	656
4,400	**4,450**	664	664	664	664
4,450	**4,500**	671	671	671	671
4,500	**4,550**	679	679	679	679
4,550	**4,600**	686	686	686	686
4,600	**4,650**	694	694	694	694
4,650	**4,700**	701	701	701	701
4,700	**4,750**	709	709	709	709
4,750	**4,800**	716	716	716	716
4,800	**4,850**	724	724	724	724
4,850	**4,900**	731	731	731	731
4,900	**4,950**	739	739	739	739
4,950	**5,000**	746	746	746	746

Continued on next page

* This column must also be used by a qualifying widow(er).

1998 Tax Table—*Continued*

If Form 1040A, line 24, is—		And you are—			
At least	But less than	Single	Married filing jointly *	Married filing sepa-rately	Head of a house-hold
		Your tax is—			
5,000					
5,000	**5,050**	754	754	754	754
5,050	**5,100**	761	761	761	761
5,100	**5,150**	769	769	769	769
5,150	**5,200**	776	776	776	776
5,200	**5,250**	784	784	784	784
5,250	**5,300**	791	791	791	791
5,300	**5,350**	799	799	799	799
5,350	**5,400**	806	806	806	806
5,400	**5,450**	814	814	814	814
5,450	**5,500**	821	821	821	821
5,500	**5,550**	829	829	829	829
5,550	**5,600**	836	836	836	836
5,600	**5,650**	844	844	844	844
5,650	**5,700**	851	851	851	851
5,700	**5,750**	859	859	859	859
5,750	**5,800**	866	866	866	866
5,800	**5,850**	874	874	874	874
5,850	**5,900**	881	881	881	881
5,900	**5,950**	889	889	889	889
5,950	**6,000**	896	896	896	896
6,000					
6,000	**6,050**	904	904	904	904
6,050	**6,100**	911	911	911	911
6,100	**6,150**	919	919	919	919
6,150	**6,200**	926	926	926	926
6,200	**6,250**	934	934	934	934
6,250	**6,300**	941	941	941	941
6,300	**6,350**	949	949	949	949
6,350	**6,400**	956	956	956	956
6,400	**6,450**	964	964	964	964
6,450	**6,500**	971	971	971	971
6,500	**6,550**	979	979	979	979
6,550	**6,600**	986	986	986	986
6,600	**6,650**	994	994	994	994
6,650	**6,700**	1,001	1,001	1,001	1,001
6,700	**6,750**	1,009	1,009	1,009	1,009
6,750	**6,800**	1,016	1,016	1,016	1,016
6,800	**6,850**	1,024	1,024	1,024	1,024
6,850	**6,900**	1,031	1,031	1,031	1,031
6,900	**6,950**	1,039	1,039	1,039	1,039
6,950	**7,000**	1,046	1,046	1,046	1,046
7,000					
7,000	**7,050**	1,054	1,054	1,054	1,054
7,050	**7,100**	1,061	1,061	1,061	1,061
7,100	**7,150**	1,069	1,069	1,069	1,069
7,150	**7,200**	1,076	1,076	1,076	1,076
7,200	**7,250**	1,084	1,084	1,084	1,084
7,250	**7,300**	1,091	1,091	1,091	1,091
7,300	**7,350**	1,099	1,099	1,099	1,099
7,350	**7,400**	1,106	1,106	1,106	1,106
7,400	**7,450**	1,114	1,114	1,114	1,114
7,450	**7,500**	1,121	1,121	1,121	1,121
7,500	**7,550**	1,129	1,129	1,129	1,129
7,550	**7,600**	1,136	1,136	1,136	1,136
7,600	**7,650**	1,144	1,144	1,144	1,144
7,650	**7,700**	1,151	1,151	1,151	1,151
7,700	**7,750**	1,159	1,159	1,159	1,159
7,750	**7,800**	1,166	1,166	1,166	1,166
7,800	**7,850**	1,174	1,174	1,174	1,174
7,850	**7,900**	1,181	1,181	1,181	1,181
7,900	**7,950**	1,189	1,189	1,189	1,189
7,950	**8,000**	1,196	1,196	1,196	1,196

If Form 1040A, line 24, is—		And you are—			
At least	But less than	Single	Married filing jointly *	Married filing sepa-rately	Head of a house-hold
		Your tax is—			
8,000					
8,000	**8,050**	1,204	1,204	1,204	1,204
8,050	**8,100**	1,211	1,211	1,211	1,211
8,100	**8,150**	1,219	1,219	1,219	1,219
8,150	**8,200**	1,226	1,226	1,226	1,226
8,200	**8,250**	1,234	1,234	1,234	1,234
8,250	**8,300**	1,241	1,241	1,241	1,241
8,300	**8,350**	1,249	1,249	1,249	1,249
8,350	**8,400**	1,256	1,256	1,256	1,256
8,400	**8,450**	1,264	1,264	1,264	1,264
8,450	**8,500**	1,271	1,271	1,271	1,271
8,500	**8,550**	1,279	1,279	1,279	1,279
8,550	**8,600**	1,286	1,286	1,286	1,286
8,600	**8,650**	1,294	1,294	1,294	1,294
8,650	**8,700**	1,301	1,301	1,301	1,301
8,700	**8,750**	1,309	1,309	1,309	1,309
8,750	**8,800**	1,316	1,316	1,316	1,316
8,800	**8,850**	1,324	1,324	1,324	1,324
8,850	**8,900**	1,331	1,331	1,331	1,331
8,900	**8,950**	1,339	1,339	1,339	1,339
8,950	**9,000**	1,346	1,346	1,346	1,346
9,000					
9,000	**9,050**	1,354	1,354	1,354	1,354
9,050	**9,100**	1,361	1,361	1,361	1,361
9,100	**9,150**	1,369	1,369	1,369	1,369
9,150	**9,200**	1,376	1,376	1,376	1,376
9,200	**9,250**	1,384	1,384	1,384	1,384
9,250	**9,300**	1,391	1,391	1,391	1,391
9,300	**9,350**	1,399	1,399	1,399	1,399
9,350	**9,400**	1,406	1,406	1,406	1,406
9,400	**9,450**	1,414	1,414	1,414	1,414
9,450	**9,500**	1,421	1,421	1,421	1,421
9,500	**9,550**	1,429	1,429	1,429	1,429
9,550	**9,600**	1,436	1,436	1,436	1,436
9,600	**9,650**	1,444	1,444	1,444	1,444
9,650	**9,700**	1,451	1,451	1,451	1,451
9,700	**9,750**	1,459	1,459	1,459	1,459
9,750	**9,800**	1,466	1,466	1,466	1,466
9,800	**9,850**	1,474	1,474	1,474	1,474
9,850	**9,900**	1,481	1,481	1,481	1,481
9,900	**9,950**	1,489	1,489	1,489	1,489
9,950	**10,000**	1,496	1,496	1,496	1,496
10,000					
10,000	**10,050**	1,504	1,504	1,504	1,504
10,050	**10,100**	1,511	1,511	1,511	1,511
10,100	**10,150**	1,519	1,519	1,519	1,519
10,150	**10,200**	1,526	1,526	1,526	1,526
10,200	**10,250**	1,534	1,534	1,534	1,534
10,250	**10,300**	1,541	1,541	1,541	1,541
10,300	**10,350**	1,549	1,549	1,549	1,549
10,350	**10,400**	1,556	1,556	1,556	1,556
10,400	**10,450**	1,564	1,564	1,564	1,564
10,450	**10,500**	1,571	1,571	1,571	1,571
10,500	**10,550**	1,579	1,579	1,579	1,579
10,550	**10,600**	1,586	1,586	1,586	1,586
10,600	**10,650**	1,594	1,594	1,594	1,594
10,650	**10,700**	1,601	1,601	1,601	1,601
10,700	**10,750**	1,609	1,609	1,609	1,609
10,750	**10,800**	1,616	1,616	1,616	1,616
10,800	**10,850**	1,624	1,624	1,624	1,624
10,850	**10,900**	1,631	1,631	1,631	1,631
10,900	**10,950**	1,639	1,639	1,639	1,639
10,950	**11,000**	1,646	1,646	1,646	1,646

If Form 1040A, line 24, is—		And you are—			
At least	But less than	Single	Married filing jointly *	Married filing sepa-rately	Head of a house-hold
		Your tax is—			
11,000					
11,000	**11,050**	1,654	1,654	1,654	1,654
11,050	**11,100**	1,661	1,661	1,661	1,661
11,100	**11,150**	1,669	1,669	1,669	1,669
11,150	**11,200**	1,676	1,676	1,676	1,676
11,200	**11,250**	1,684	1,684	1,684	1,684
11,250	**11,300**	1,691	1,691	1,691	1,691
11,300	**11,350**	1,699	1,699	1,699	1,699
11,350	**11,400**	1,706	1,706	1,706	1,706
11,400	**11,450**	1,714	1,714	1,714	1,714
11,450	**11,500**	1,721	1,721	1,721	1,721
11,500	**11,550**	1,729	1,729	1,729	1,729
11,550	**11,600**	1,736	1,736	1,736	1,736
11,600	**11,650**	1,744	1,744	1,744	1,744
11,650	**11,700**	1,751	1,751	1,751	1,751
11,700	**11,750**	1,759	1,759	1,759	1,759
11,750	**11,800**	1,766	1,766	1,766	1,766
11,800	**11,850**	1,774	1,774	1,774	1,774
11,850	**11,900**	1,781	1,781	1,781	1,781
11,900	**11,950**	1,789	1,789	1,789	1,789
11,950	**12,000**	1,796	1,796	1,796	1,796
12,000					
12,000	**12,050**	1,804	1,804	1,804	1,804
12,050	**12,100**	1,811	1,811	1,811	1,811
12,100	**12,150**	1,819	1,819	1,819	1,819
12,150	**12,200**	1,826	1,826	1,826	1,826
12,200	**12,250**	1,834	1,834	1,834	1,834
12,250	**12,300**	1,841	1,841	1,841	1,841
12,300	**12,350**	1,849	1,849	1,849	1,849
12,350	**12,400**	1,856	1,856	1,856	1,856
12,400	**12,450**	1,864	1,864	1,864	1,864
12,450	**12,500**	1,871	1,871	1,871	1,871
12,500	**12,550**	1,879	1,879	1,879	1,879
12,550	**12,600**	1,886	1,886	1,886	1,886
12,600	**12,650**	1,894	1,894	1,894	1,894
12,650	**12,700**	1,901	1,901	1,901	1,901
12,700	**12,750**	1,909	1,909	1,909	1,909
12,750	**12,800**	1,916	1,916	1,916	1,916
12,800	**12,850**	1,924	1,924	1,924	1,924
12,850	**12,900**	1,931	1,931	1,931	1,931
12,900	**12,950**	1,939	1,939	1,939	1,939
12,950	**13,000**	1,946	1,946	1,946	1,946
13,000					
13,000	**13,050**	1,954	1,954	1,954	1,954
13,050	**13,100**	1,961	1,961	1,961	1,961
13,100	**13,150**	1,969	1,969	1,969	1,969
13,150	**13,200**	1,976	1,976	1,976	1,976
13,200	**13,250**	1,984	1,984	1,984	1,984
13,250	**13,300**	1,991	1,991	1,991	1,991
13,300	**13,350**	1,999	1,999	1,999	1,999
13,350	**13,400**	2,006	2,006	2,006	2,006
13,400	**13,450**	2,014	2,014	2,014	2,014
13,450	**13,500**	2,021	2,021	2,021	2,021
13,500	**13,550**	2,029	2,029	2,029	2,029
13,550	**13,600**	2,036	2,036	2,036	2,036
13,600	**13,650**	2,044	2,044	2,044	2,044
13,650	**13,700**	2,051	2,051	2,051	2,051
13,700	**13,750**	2,059	2,059	2,059	2,059
13,750	**13,800**	2,066	2,066	2,066	2,066
13,800	**13,850**	2,074	2,074	2,074	2,074
13,850	**13,900**	2,081	2,081	2,081	2,081
13,900	**13,950**	2,089	2,089	2,089	2,089
13,950	**14,000**	2,096	2,096	2,096	2,096

* This column must also be used by a qualifying widow(er).

Continued on next page

1998 Tax Table—*Continued*

If Form 1040A, line 24, is—		And you are—				If Form 1040A, line 24, is—		And you are—				If Form 1040A, line 24, is—		And you are—			
At least	But less than	Single	Married filing jointly *	Married filing separately	Head of a household	At least	But less than	Single	Married filing jointly *	Married filing separately	Head of a household	At least	But less than	Single	Married filing jointly *	Married filing separately	Head of a household
		Your tax is—						Your tax is—						Your tax is—			
14,000						**17,000**						**20,000**					
14,000	**14,050**	2,104	2,104	2,104	2,104	**17,000**	**17,050**	2,554	2,554	2,554	2,554	**20,000**	**20,050**	3,004	3,004	3,004	3,004
14,050	**14,100**	2,111	2,111	2,111	2,111	**17,050**	**17,100**	2,561	2,561	2,561	2,561	**20,050**	**20,100**	3,011	3,011	3,011	3,011
14,100	**14,150**	2,119	2,119	2,119	2,119	**17,100**	**17,150**	2,569	2,569	2,569	2,569	**20,100**	**20,150**	3,019	3,019	3,019	3,019
14,150	**14,200**	2,126	2,126	2,126	2,126	**17,150**	**17,200**	2,576	2,576	2,576	2,576	**20,150**	**20,200**	3,026	3,026	3,026	3,026
14,200	**14,250**	2,134	2,134	2,134	2,134	**17,200**	**17,250**	2,584	2,584	2,584	2,584	**20,200**	**20,250**	3,034	3,034	3,034	3,034
14,250	**14,300**	2,141	2,141	2,141	2,141	**17,250**	**17,300**	2,591	2,591	2,591	2,591	**20,250**	**20,300**	3,041	3,041	3,041	3,041
14,300	**14,350**	2,149	2,149	2,149	2,149	**17,300**	**17,350**	2,599	2,599	2,599	2,599	**20,300**	**20,350**	3,049	3,049	3,049	3,049
14,350	**14,400**	2,156	2,156	2,156	2,156	**17,350**	**17,400**	2,606	2,606	2,606	2,606	**20,350**	**20,400**	3,056	3,056	3,056	3,056
14,400	**14,450**	2,164	2,164	2,164	2,164	**17,400**	**17,450**	2,614	2,614	2,614	2,614	**20,400**	**20,450**	3,064	3,064	3,064	3,064
14,450	**14,500**	2,171	2,171	2,171	2,171	**17,450**	**17,500**	2,621	2,621	2,621	2,621	**20,450**	**20,500**	3,071	3,071	3,071	3,071
14,500	**14,550**	2,179	2,179	2,179	2,179	**17,500**	**17,550**	2,629	2,629	2,629	2,629	**20,500**	**20,550**	3,079	3,079	3,079	3,079
14,550	**14,600**	2,186	2,186	2,186	2,186	**17,550**	**17,600**	2,636	2,636	2,636	2,636	**20,550**	**20,600**	3,086	3,086	3,086	3,086
14,600	**14,650**	2,194	2,194	2,194	2,194	**17,600**	**17,650**	2,644	2,644	2,644	2,644	**20,600**	**20,650**	3,094	3,094	3,094	3,094
14,650	**14,700**	2,201	2,201	2,201	2,201	**17,650**	**17,700**	2,651	2,651	2,651	2,651	**20,650**	**20,700**	3,101	3,101	3,101	3,101
14,700	**14,750**	2,209	2,209	2,209	2,209	**17,700**	**17,750**	2,659	2,659	2,659	2,659	**20,700**	**20,750**	3,109	3,109	3,109	3,109
14,750	**14,800**	2,216	2,216	2,216	2,216	**17,750**	**17,800**	2,666	2,666	2,666	2,666	**20,750**	**20,800**	3,116	3,116	3,116	3,116
14,800	**14,850**	2,224	2,224	2,224	2,224	**17,800**	**17,850**	2,674	2,674	2,674	2,674	**20,800**	**20,850**	3,124	3,124	3,124	3,124
14,850	**14,900**	2,231	2,231	2,231	2,231	**17,850**	**17,900**	2,681	2,681	2,681	2,681	**20,850**	**20,900**	3,131	3,131	3,131	3,131
14,900	**14,950**	2,239	2,239	2,239	2,239	**17,900**	**17,950**	2,689	2,689	2,689	2,689	**20,900**	**20,950**	3,139	3,139	3,139	3,139
14,950	**15,000**	2,246	2,246	2,246	2,246	**17,950**	**18,000**	2,696	2,696	2,696	2,696	**20,950**	**21,000**	3,146	3,146	3,146	3,146
15,000						**18,000**						**21,000**					
15,000	**15,050**	2,254	2,254	2,254	2,254	**18,000**	**18,050**	2,704	2,704	2,704	2,704	**21,000**	**21,050**	3,154	3,154	3,154	3,154
15,050	**15,100**	2,261	2,261	2,261	2,261	**18,050**	**18,100**	2,711	2,711	2,711	2,711	**21,050**	**21,100**	3,161	3,161	3,161	3,161
15,100	**15,150**	2,269	2,269	2,269	2,269	**18,100**	**18,150**	2,719	2,719	2,719	2,719	**21,100**	**21,150**	3,169	3,169	3,169	3,169
15,150	**15,200**	2,276	2,276	2,276	2,276	**18,150**	**18,200**	2,726	2,726	2,726	2,726	**21,150**	**21,200**	3,176	3,176	3,176	3,176
15,200	**15,250**	2,284	2,284	2,284	2,284	**18,200**	**18,250**	2,734	2,734	2,734	2,734	**21,200**	**21,250**	3,184	3,184	3,190	3,184
15,250	**15,300**	2,291	2,291	2,291	2,291	**18,250**	**18,300**	2,741	2,741	2,741	2,741	**21,250**	**21,300**	3,191	3,191	3,204	3,191
15,300	**15,350**	2,299	2,299	2,299	2,299	**18,300**	**18,350**	2,749	2,749	2,749	2,749	**21,300**	**21,350**	3,199	3,199	3,218	3,199
15,350	**15,400**	2,306	2,306	2,306	2,306	**18,350**	**18,400**	2,756	2,756	2,756	2,756	**21,350**	**21,400**	3,206	3,206	3,232	3,206
15,400	**15,450**	2,314	2,314	2,314	2,314	**18,400**	**18,450**	2,764	2,764	2,764	2,764	**21,400**	**21,450**	3,214	3,214	3,246	3,214
15,450	**15,500**	2,321	2,321	2,321	2,321	**18,450**	**18,500**	2,771	2,771	2,771	2,771	**21,450**	**21,500**	3,221	3,221	3,260	3,221
15,500	**15,550**	2,329	2,329	2,329	2,329	**18,500**	**18,550**	2,779	2,779	2,779	2,779	**21,500**	**21,550**	3,229	3,229	3,274	3,229
15,550	**15,600**	2,336	2,336	2,336	2,336	**18,550**	**18,600**	2,786	2,786	2,786	2,786	**21,550**	**21,600**	3,236	3,236	3,288	3,236
15,600	**15,650**	2,344	2,344	2,344	2,344	**18,600**	**18,650**	2,794	2,794	2,794	2,794	**21,600**	**21,650**	3,244	3,244	3,302	3,244
15,650	**15,700**	2,351	2,351	2,351	2,351	**18,650**	**18,700**	2,801	2,801	2,801	2,801	**21,650**	**21,700**	3,251	3,251	3,316	3,251
15,700	**15,750**	2,359	2,359	2,359	2,359	**18,700**	**18,750**	2,809	2,809	2,809	2,809	**21,700**	**21,750**	3,259	3,259	3,330	3,259
15,750	**15,800**	2,366	2,366	2,366	2,366	**18,750**	**18,800**	2,816	2,816	2,816	2,816	**21,750**	**21,800**	3,266	3,266	3,344	3,266
15,800	**15,850**	2,374	2,374	2,374	2,374	**18,800**	**18,850**	2,824	2,824	2,824	2,824	**21,800**	**21,850**	3,274	3,274	3,358	3,274
15,850	**15,900**	2,381	2,381	2,381	2,381	**18,850**	**18,900**	2,831	2,831	2,831	2,831	**21,850**	**21,900**	3,281	3,281	3,372	3,281
15,900	**15,950**	2,389	2,389	2,389	2,389	**18,900**	**18,950**	2,839	2,839	2,839	2,839	**21,900**	**21,950**	3,289	3,289	3,386	3,289
15,950	**16,000**	2,396	2,396	2,396	2,396	**18,950**	**19,000**	2,846	2,846	2,846	2,846	**21,950**	**22,000**	3,296	3,296	3,400	3,296
16,000						**19,000**						**22,000**					
16,000	**16,050**	2,404	2,404	2,404	2,404	**19,000**	**19,050**	2,854	2,854	2,854	2,854	**22,000**	**22,050**	3,304	3,304	3,414	3,304
16,050	**16,100**	2,411	2,411	2,411	2,411	**19,050**	**19,100**	2,861	2,861	2,861	2,861	**22,050**	**22,100**	3,311	3,311	3,428	3,311
16,100	**16,150**	2,419	2,419	2,419	2,419	**19,100**	**19,150**	2,869	2,869	2,869	2,869	**22,100**	**22,150**	3,319	3,319	3,442	3,319
16,150	**16,200**	2,426	2,426	2,426	2,426	**19,150**	**19,200**	2,876	2,876	2,876	2,876	**22,150**	**22,200**	3,326	3,326	3,456	3,326
16,200	**16,250**	2,434	2,434	2,434	2,434	**19,200**	**19,250**	2,884	2,884	2,884	2,884	**22,200**	**22,250**	3,334	3,334	3,470	3,334
16,250	**16,300**	2,441	2,441	2,441	2,441	**19,250**	**19,300**	2,891	2,891	2,891	2,891	**22,250**	**22,300**	3,341	3,341	3,484	3,341
16,300	**16,350**	2,449	2,449	2,449	2,449	**19,300**	**19,350**	2,899	2,899	2,899	2,899	**22,300**	**22,350**	3,349	3,349	3,498	3,349
16,350	**16,400**	2,456	2,456	2,456	2,456	**19,350**	**19,400**	2,906	2,906	2,906	2,906	**22,350**	**22,400**	3,356	3,356	3,512	3,356
16,400	**16,450**	2,464	2,464	2,464	2,464	**19,400**	**19,450**	2,914	2,914	2,914	2,914	**22,400**	**22,450**	3,364	3,364	3,526	3,364
16,450	**16,500**	2,471	2,471	2,471	2,471	**19,450**	**19,500**	2,921	2,921	2,921	2,921	**22,450**	**22,500**	3,371	3,371	3,540	3,371
16,500	**16,550**	2,479	2,479	2,479	2,479	**19,500**	**19,550**	2,929	2,929	2,929	2,929	**22,500**	**22,550**	3,379	3,379	3,554	3,379
16,550	**16,600**	2,486	2,486	2,486	2,486	**19,550**	**19,600**	2,936	2,936	2,936	2,936	**22,550**	**22,600**	3,386	3,386	3,568	3,386
16,600	**16,650**	2,494	2,494	2,494	2,494	**19,600**	**19,650**	2,944	2,944	2,944	2,944	**22,600**	**22,650**	3,394	3,394	3,582	3,394
16,650	**16,700**	2,501	2,501	2,501	2,501	**19,650**	**19,700**	2,951	2,951	2,951	2,951	**22,650**	**22,700**	3,401	3,401	3,596	3,401
16,700	**16,750**	2,509	2,509	2,509	2,509	**19,700**	**19,750**	2,959	2,959	2,959	2,959	**22,700**	**22,750**	3,409	3,409	3,610	3,409
16,750	**16,800**	2,516	2,516	2,516	2,516	**19,750**	**19,800**	2,966	2,966	2,966	2,966	**22,750**	**22,800**	3,416	3,416	3,624	3,416
16,800	**16,850**	2,524	2,524	2,524	2,524	**19,800**	**19,850**	2,974	2,974	2,974	2,974	**22,800**	**22,850**	3,424	3,424	3,638	3,424
16,850	**16,900**	2,531	2,531	2,531	2,531	**19,850**	**19,900**	2,981	2,981	2,981	2,981	**22,850**	**22,900**	3,431	3,431	3,652	3,431
16,900	**16,950**	2,539	2,539	2,539	2,539	**19,900**	**19,950**	2,989	2,989	2,989	2,989	**22,900**	**22,950**	3,439	3,439	3,666	3,439
16,950	**17,000**	2,546	2,546	2,546	2,546	**19,950**	**20,000**	2,996	2,996	2,996	2,996	**22,950**	**23,000**	3,446	3,446	3,680	3,446

* This column must also be used by a qualifying widow(er).

Continued on next page

1998 Tax Table—*Continued*

If Form 1040A, line 24, is—		And you are—			
At least	But less than	Single	Married filing jointly *	Married filing sepa-rately	Head of a house-hold
		Your tax is—			
23,000					
23,000	**23,050**	3,454	3,454	3,694	3,454
23,050	**23,100**	3,461	3,461	3,708	3,461
23,100	**23,150**	3,469	3,469	3,722	3,469
23,150	**23,200**	3,476	3,476	3,736	3,476
23,200	**23,250**	3,484	3,484	3,750	3,484
23,250	**23,300**	3,491	3,491	3,764	3,491
23,300	**23,350**	3,499	3,499	3,778	3,499
23,350	**23,400**	3,506	3,506	3,792	3,506
23,400	**23,450**	3,514	3,514	3,806	3,514
23,450	**23,500**	3,521	3,521	3,820	3,521
23,500	**23,550**	3,529	3,529	3,834	3,529
23,550	**23,600**	3,536	3,536	3,848	3,536
23,600	**23,650**	3,544	3,544	3,862	3,544
23,650	**23,700**	3,551	3,551	3,876	3,551
23,700	**23,750**	3,559	3,559	3,890	3,559
23,750	**23,800**	3,566	3,566	3,904	3,566
23,800	**23,850**	3,574	3,574	3,918	3,574
23,850	**23,900**	3,581	3,581	3,932	3,581
23,900	**23,950**	3,589	3,589	3,946	3,589
23,950	**24,000**	3,596	3,596	3,960	3,596
24,000					
24,000	**24,050**	3,604	3,604	3,974	3,604
24,050	**24,100**	3,611	3,611	3,988	3,611
24,100	**24,150**	3,619	3,619	4,002	3,619
24,150	**24,200**	3,626	3,626	4,016	3,626
24,200	**24,250**	3,634	3,634	4,030	3,634
24,250	**24,300**	3,641	3,641	4,044	3,641
24,300	**24,350**	3,649	3,649	4,058	3,649
24,350	**24,400**	3,656	3,656	4,072	3,656
24,400	**24,450**	3,664	3,664	4,086	3,664
24,450	**24,500**	3,671	3,671	4,100	3,671
24,500	**24,550**	3,679	3,679	4,114	3,679
24,550	**24,600**	3,686	3,686	4,128	3,686
24,600	**24,650**	3,694	3,694	4,142	3,694
24,650	**24,700**	3,701	3,701	4,156	3,701
24,700	**24,750**	3,709	3,709	4,170	3,709
24,750	**24,800**	3,716	3,716	4,184	3,716
24,800	**24,850**	3,724	3,724	4,198	3,724
24,850	**24,900**	3,731	3,731	4,212	3,731
24,900	**24,950**	3,739	3,739	4,226	3,739
24,950	**25,000**	3,746	3,746	4,240	3,746
25,000					
25,000	**25,050**	3,754	3,754	4,254	3,754
25,050	**25,100**	3,761	3,761	4,268	3,761
25,100	**25,150**	3,769	3,769	4,282	3,769
25,150	**25,200**	3,776	3,776	4,296	3,776
25,200	**25,250**	3,784	3,784	4,310	3,784
25,250	**25,300**	3,791	3,791	4,324	3,791
25,300	**25,350**	3,799	3,799	4,338	3,799
25,350	**25,400**	3,810	3,806	4,352	3,806
25,400	**25,450**	3,824	3,814	4,366	3,814
25,450	**25,500**	3,838	3,821	4,380	3,821
25,500	**25,550**	3,852	3,829	4,394	3,829
25,550	**25,600**	3,866	3,836	4,408	3,836
25,600	**25,650**	3,880	3,844	[illegible]	[illegible]
25,650	**25,700**	3,894	3,851	4,436	3,851
25,700	**25,750**	3,908	3,859	4,450	3,859
25,750	**25,800**	3,922	3,866	4,464	3,866
25,800	**25,850**	3,936	3,874	4,478	3,874
25,850	**25,900**	3,950	3,881	4,492	3,881
25,900	**25,950**	3,964	3,889	4,506	3,889
25,950	**26,000**	3,978	3,896	4,520	3,896
26,000					
26,000	**26,050**	3,992	3,904	4,534	3,904
26,050	**26,100**	4,006	3,911	4,548	3,911
26,100	**26,150**	4,020	3,919	4,562	3,919
26,150	**26,200**	4,034	3,926	4,576	3,926
26,200	**26,250**	4,048	3,934	4,590	3,934
26,250	**26,300**	4,062	3,941	4,604	3,941
26,300	**26,350**	4,076	3,949	4,618	3,949
26,350	**26,400**	4,090	3,956	4,632	3,956
26,400	**26,450**	4,104	3,964	4,646	3,964
26,450	**26,500**	4,118	3,971	4,660	3,971
26,500	**26,550**	4,132	3,979	4,674	3,979
26,550	**26,600**	4,146	3,986	4,688	3,986
26,600	**26,650**	4,160	3,994	4,702	3,994
26,650	**26,700**	4,174	4,001	4,716	4,001
26,700	**26,750**	4,188	4,009	4,730	4,009
26,750	**26,800**	4,202	4,016	4,744	4,016
26,800	**26,850**	4,216	4,024	4,758	4,024
26,850	**26,900**	4,230	4,031	4,772	4,031
26,900	**26,950**	4,244	4,039	4,786	4,039
26,950	**27,000**	4,258	4,046	4,800	4,046
27,000					
27,000	**27,050**	4,272	4,054	4,814	4,054
27,050	**27,100**	4,286	4,061	4,828	4,061
27,100	**27,150**	4,300	4,069	4,842	4,069
27,150	**27,200**	4,314	4,076	4,856	4,076
27,200	**27,250**	4,328	4,084	4,870	4,084
27,250	**27,300**	4,342	4,091	4,884	4,091
27,300	**27,350**	4,356	4,099	4,898	4,099
27,350	**27,400**	4,370	4,106	4,912	4,106
27,400	**27,450**	4,384	4,114	4,926	4,114
27,450	**27,500**	4,398	4,121	4,940	4,121
27,500	**27,550**	4,412	4,129	4,954	4,129
27,550	**27,600**	4,426	4,136	4,968	4,136
27,600	**27,650**	4,440	4,144	4,982	4,144
27,650	**27,700**	4,454	4,151	4,996	4,151
27,700	**27,750**	4,468	4,159	5,010	4,159
27,750	**27,800**	4,482	4,166	5,024	4,166
27,800	**27,850**	4,496	4,174	5,038	4,174
27,850	**27,900**	4,510	4,181	5,052	4,181
27,900	**27,950**	4,524	4,189	5,066	4,189
27,950	**28,000**	4,538	4,196	5,080	4,196
28,000					
28,000	**28,050**	4,552	4,204	5,094	4,204
28,050	**28,100**	4,566	4,211	5,108	4,211
28,100	**28,150**	4,580	4,219	5,122	4,219
28,150	**28,200**	4,594	4,226	5,136	4,226
28,200	**28,250**	4,608	4,234	5,150	4,234
28,250	**28,300**	4,622	4,241	5,164	4,241
28,300	**28,350**	4,636	4,249	5,178	4,249
28,350	**28,400**	4,650	4,256	5,192	4,256
28,400	**28,450**	4,664	4,264	5,206	4,264
28,450	**28,500**	4,678	4,271	5,220	4,271
28,500	**28,550**	4,692	4,279	5,234	4,279
28,550	**28,600**	4,706	4,286	5,248	4,286
[illegible]	**28,650**	4,720	4,294	5,262	4,294
28,650	**28,700**	4,734	4,301	5,276	4,301
28,700	**28,750**	4,748	4,309	5,290	4,309
28,750	**28,800**	4,762	4,316	5,304	4,316
28,800	**28,850**	4,776	4,324	5,318	4,324
28,850	**28,900**	4,790	4,331	5,332	4,331
28,900	**28,950**	4,804	4,339	5,346	4,339
28,950	**29,000**	4,818	4,346	5,360	4,346
29,000					
29,000	**29,050**	4,832	4,354	5,374	4,354
29,050	**29,100**	4,846	4,361	5,388	4,361
29,100	**29,150**	4,860	4,369	5,402	4,369
29,150	**29,200**	4,874	4,376	5,416	4,376
29,200	**29,250**	4,888	4,384	5,430	4,384
29,250	**29,300**	4,902	4,391	5,444	4,391
29,300	**29,350**	4,916	4,399	5,458	4,399
29,350	**29,400**	4,930	4,406	5,472	4,406
29,400	**29,450**	4,944	4,414	5,486	4,414
29,450	**29,500**	4,958	4,421	5,500	4,421
29,500	**29,550**	4,972	4,429	5,514	4,429
29,550	**29,600**	4,986	4,436	5,528	4,436
29,600	**29,650**	5,000	4,444	5,542	4,444
29,650	**29,700**	5,014	4,451	5,556	4,451
29,700	**29,750**	5,028	4,459	5,570	4,459
29,750	**29,800**	5,042	4,466	5,584	4,466
29,800	**29,850**	5,056	4,474	5,598	4,474
29,850	**29,900**	5,070	4,481	5,612	4,481
29,900	**29,950**	5,084	4,489	5,626	4,489
29,950	**30,000**	5,098	4,496	5,640	4,496
30,000					
30,000	**30,050**	5,112	4,504	5,654	4,504
30,050	**30,100**	5,126	4,511	5,668	4,511
30,100	**30,150**	5,140	4,519	5,682	4,519
30,150	**30,200**	5,154	4,526	5,696	4,526
30,200	**30,250**	5,168	4,534	5,710	4,534
30,250	**30,300**	5,182	4,541	5,724	4,541
30,300	**30,350**	5,196	4,549	5,738	4,549
30,350	**30,400**	5,210	4,556	5,752	4,556
30,400	**30,450**	5,224	4,564	5,766	4,564
30,450	**30,500**	5,238	4,571	5,780	4,571
30,500	**30,550**	5,252	4,579	5,794	4,579
30,550	**30,600**	5,266	4,586	5,808	4,586
30,600	**30,650**	5,280	4,594	5,822	4,594
30,650	**30,700**	5,294	4,601	5,836	4,601
30,700	**30,750**	5,308	4,609	5,850	4,609
30,750	**30,800**	5,322	4,616	5,864	4,616
30,800	**30,850**	5,336	4,624	5,878	4,624
30,850	**30,900**	5,350	4,631	5,892	4,631
30,900	**30,950**	5,364	4,639	5,906	4,639
30,950	**31,000**	5,378	4,646	5,920	4,646
31,000					
31,000	**31,050**	5,392	4,654	5,934	4,654
31,050	**31,100**	5,406	4,661	5,948	4,661
31,100	**31,150**	5,420	4,669	5,962	4,669
31,150	**31,200**	5,434	4,676	5,976	4,676
31,200	**31,250**	5,448	4,684	5,990	4,684
31,250	**31,300**	5,462	4,691	6,004	4,691
31,300	**31,350**	5,476	4,699	6,018	4,699
31,350	**31,400**	5,490	4,706	6,032	4,706
31,400	**31,450**	5,504	4,714	6,046	4,714
31,450	**31,500**	5,518	4,721	6,060	4,721
31,500	**31,550**	5,532	4,729	6,074	4,729
31,550	**31,600**	5,546	[illegible]	[illegible]	[illegible]
31,600	**31,650**	5,560	4,744	6,102	4,744
31,650	**31,700**	5,574	4,751	6,116	4,751
31,700	**31,750**	5,588	4,759	6,130	4,759
31,750	**31,800**	5,602	4,766	6,144	4,766
31,800	**31,850**	5,616	4,774	6,158	4,774
31,850	**31,900**	5,630	4,781	6,172	4,781
31,900	**31,950**	5,644	4,789	6,186	4,789
31,950	**32,000**	5,658	4,796	6,200	4,796

* This column must also be used by a qualifying widow(er).

Continued on next page

1998 Tax Table—*Continued*

If Form 1040A, line 24, is—		And you are—			
At least	But less than	Single	Married filing jointly *	Married filing sepa-rately	Head of a house-hold
		Your tax is—			
32,000					
32,000	**32,050**	5,672	4,804	6,214	4,804
32,050	**32,100**	5,686	4,811	6,228	4,811
32,100	**32,150**	5,700	4,819	6,242	4,819
32,150	**32,200**	5,714	4,826	6,256	4,826
32,200	**32,250**	5,728	4,834	6,270	4,834
32,250	**32,300**	5,742	4,841	6,284	4,841
32,300	**32,350**	5,756	4,849	6,298	4,849
32,350	**32,400**	5,770	4,856	6,312	4,856
32,400	**32,450**	5,784	4,864	6,326	4,864
32,450	**32,500**	5,798	4,871	6,340	4,871
32,500	**32,550**	5,812	4,879	6,354	4,879
32,550	**32,600**	5,826	4,886	6,368	4,886
32,600	**32,650**	5,840	4,894	6,382	4,894
32,650	**32,700**	5,854	4,901	6,396	4,901
32,700	**32,750**	5,868	4,909	6,410	4,909
32,750	**32,800**	5,882	4,916	6,424	4,916
32,800	**32,850**	5,896	4,924	6,438	4,924
32,850	**32,900**	5,910	4,931	6,452	4,931
32,900	**32,950**	5,924	4,939	6,466	4,939
32,950	**33,000**	5,938	4,946	6,480	4,946
33,000					
33,000	**33,050**	5,952	4,954	6,494	4,954
33,050	**33,100**	5,966	4,961	6,508	4,961
33,100	**33,150**	5,980	4,969	6,522	4,969
33,150	**33,200**	5,994	4,976	6,536	4,976
33,200	**33,250**	6,008	4,984	6,550	4,984
33,250	**33,300**	6,022	4,991	6,564	4,991
33,300	**33,350**	6,036	4,999	6,578	4,999
33,350	**33,400**	6,050	5,006	6,592	5,006
33,400	**33,450**	6,064	5,014	6,606	5,014
33,450	**33,500**	6,078	5,021	6,620	5,021
33,500	**33,550**	6,092	5,029	6,634	5,029
33,550	**33,600**	6,106	5,036	6,648	5,036
33,600	**33,650**	6,120	5,044	6,662	5,044
33,650	**33,700**	6,134	5,051	6,676	5,051
33,700	**33,750**	6,148	5,059	6,690	5,059
33,750	**33,800**	6,162	5,066	6,704	5,066
33,800	**33,850**	6,176	5,074	6,718	5,074
33,850	**33,900**	6,190	5,081	6,732	5,081
33,900	**33,950**	6,204	5,089	6,746	5,089
33,950	**34,000**	6,218	5,096	6,760	5,100
34,000					
34,000	**34,050**	6,232	5,104	6,774	5,114
34,050	**34,100**	6,246	5,111	6,788	5,128
34,100	**34,150**	6,260	5,119	6,802	5,142
34,150	**34,200**	6,274	5,126	6,816	5,156
34,200	**34,250**	6,288	5,134	6,830	5,170
34,250	**34,300**	6,302	5,141	6,844	5,184
34,300	**34,350**	6,316	5,149	6,858	5,198
34,350	**34,400**	6,330	5,156	6,872	5,212
34,400	**34,450**	6,344	5,164	6,886	5,226
34,450	**34,500**	6,358	5,171	6,900	5,240
34,500	**34,550**	6,372	5,179	6,914	5,254
34,550	**34,600**	6,386	5,186	6,928	5,268
34,600	**34,650**	6,400	5,194	6,942	5,282
34,650	**34,700**	6,414	5,201	6,956	5,296
34,700	**34,750**	6,428	5,209	6,970	5,310
34,750	**34,800**	6,442	5,216	6,984	5,324
34,800	**34,850**	6,456	5,224	6,998	5,338
34,850	**34,900**	6,470	5,231	7,012	5,352
34,900	**34,950**	6,484	5,239	7,026	5,366
34,950	**35,000**	6,498	5,246	7,040	5,380

If Form 1040A, line 24, is—		And you are—			
At least	But less than	Single	Married filing jointly *	Married filing sepa-rately	Head of a house-hold
		Your tax is—			
35,000					
35,000	**35,050**	6,512	5,254	7,054	5,394
35,050	**35,100**	6,526	5,261	7,068	5,408
35,100	**35,150**	6,540	5,269	7,082	5,422
35,150	**35,200**	6,554	5,276	7,096	5,436
35,200	**35,250**	6,568	5,284	7,110	5,450
35,250	**35,300**	6,582	5,291	7,124	5,464
35,300	**35,350**	6,596	5,299	7,138	5,478
35,350	**35,400**	6,610	5,306	7,152	5,492
35,400	**35,450**	6,624	5,314	7,166	5,506
35,450	**35,500**	6,638	5,321	7,180	5,520
35,500	**35,550**	6,652	5,329	7,194	5,534
35,550	**35,600**	6,666	5,336	7,208	5,548
35,600	**35,650**	6,680	5,344	7,222	5,562
35,650	**35,700**	6,694	5,351	7,236	5,576
35,700	**35,750**	6,708	5,359	7,250	5,590
35,750	**35,800**	6,722	5,366	7,264	5,604
35,800	**35,850**	6,736	5,374	7,278	5,618
35,850	**35,900**	6,750	5,381	7,292	5,632
35,900	**35,950**	6,764	5,389	7,306	5,646
35,950	**36,000**	6,778	5,396	7,320	5,660
36,000					
36,000	**36,050**	6,792	5,404	7,334	5,674
36,050	**36,100**	6,806	5,411	7,348	5,688
36,100	**36,150**	6,820	5,419	7,362	5,702
36,150	**36,200**	6,834	5,426	7,376	5,716
36,200	**36,250**	6,848	5,434	7,390	5,730
36,250	**36,300**	6,862	5,441	7,404	5,744
36,300	**36,350**	6,876	5,449	7,418	5,758
36,350	**36,400**	6,890	5,456	7,432	5,772
36,400	**36,450**	6,904	5,464	7,446	5,786
36,450	**36,500**	6,918	5,471	7,460	5,800
36,500	**36,550**	6,932	5,479	7,474	5,814
36,550	**36,600**	6,946	5,486	7,488	5,828
36,600	**36,650**	6,960	5,494	7,502	5,842
36,650	**36,700**	6,974	5,501	7,516	5,856
36,700	**36,750**	6,988	5,509	7,530	5,870
36,750	**36,800**	7,002	5,516	7,544	5,884
36,800	**36,850**	7,016	5,524	7,558	5,898
36,850	**36,900**	7,030	5,531	7,572	5,912
36,900	**36,950**	7,044	5,539	7,586	5,926
36,950	**37,000**	7,058	5,546	7,600	5,940
37,000					
37,000	**37,050**	7,072	5,554	7,614	5,954
37,050	**37,100**	7,086	5,561	7,628	5,968
37,100	**37,150**	7,100	5,569	7,642	5,982
37,150	**37,200**	7,114	5,576	7,656	5,996
37,200	**37,250**	7,128	5,584	7,670	6,010
37,250	**37,300**	7,142	5,591	7,684	6,024
37,300	**37,350**	7,156	5,599	7,698	6,038
37,350	**37,400**	7,170	5,606	7,712	6,052
37,400	**37,450**	7,184	5,614	7,726	6,066
37,450	**37,500**	7,198	5,621	7,740	6,080
37,500	**37,550**	7,212	5,629	7,754	6,094
37,550	**37,600**	7,226	5,636	7,768	6,108
37,600	**37,650**	7,240	5,644	7,782	6,122
37,650	**37,700**	7,254	5,651	7,796	6,136
37,700	**37,750**	7,268	5,659	7,810	6,150
37,750	**37,800**	7,282	5,666	7,824	6,164
37,800	**37,850**	7,296	5,674	7,838	6,178
37,850	**37,900**	7,310	5,681	7,852	6,192
37,900	**37,950**	7,324	5,689	7,866	6,206
37,950	**38,000**	7,338	5,696	7,880	6,220

If Form 1040A, line 24, is—		And you are—			
At least	But less than	Single	Married filing jointly *	Married filing sepa-rately	Head of a house-hold
		Your tax is—			
38,000					
38,000	**38,050**	7,352	5,704	7,894	6,234
38,050	**38,100**	7,366	5,711	7,908	6,248
38,100	**38,150**	7,380	5,719	7,922	6,262
38,150	**38,200**	7,394	5,726	7,936	6,276
38,200	**38,250**	7,408	5,734	7,950	6,290
38,250	**38,300**	7,422	5,741	7,964	6,304
38,300	**38,350**	7,436	5,749	7,978	6,318
38,350	**38,400**	7,450	5,756	7,992	6,332
38,400	**38,450**	7,464	5,764	8,006	6,346
38,450	**38,500**	7,478	5,771	8,020	6,360
38,500	**38,550**	7,492	5,779	8,034	6,374
38,550	**38,600**	7,506	5,786	8,048	6,388
38,600	**38,650**	7,520	5,794	8,062	6,402
38,650	**38,700**	7,534	5,801	8,076	6,416
38,700	**38,750**	7,548	5,809	8,090	6,430
38,750	**38,800**	7,562	5,816	8,104	6,444
38,800	**38,850**	7,576	5,824	8,118	6,458
38,850	**38,900**	7,590	5,831	8,132	6,472
38,900	**38,950**	7,604	5,839	8,146	6,486
38,950	**39,000**	7,618	5,846	8,160	6,500
39,000					
39,000	**39,050**	7,632	5,854	8,174	6,514
39,050	**39,100**	7,646	5,861	8,188	6,528
39,100	**39,150**	7,660	5,869	8,202	6,542
39,150	**39,200**	7,674	5,876	8,216	6,556
39,200	**39,250**	7,688	5,884	8,230	6,570
39,250	**39,300**	7,702	5,891	8,244	6,584
39,300	**39,350**	7,716	5,899	8,258	6,598
39,350	**39,400**	7,730	5,906	8,272	6,612
39,400	**39,450**	7,744	5,914	8,286	6,626
39,450	**39,500**	7,758	5,921	8,300	6,640
39,500	**39,550**	7,772	5,929	8,314	6,654
39,550	**39,600**	7,786	5,936	8,328	6,668
39,600	**39,650**	7,800	5,944	8,342	6,682
39,650	**39,700**	7,814	5,951	8,356	6,696
39,700	**39,750**	7,828	5,959	8,370	6,710
39,750	**39,800**	7,842	5,966	8,384	6,724
39,800	**39,850**	7,856	5,974	8,398	6,738
39,850	**39,900**	7,870	5,981	8,412	6,752
39,900	**39,950**	7,884	5,989	8,426	6,766
39,950	**40,000**	7,898	5,996	8,440	6,780
40,000					
40,000	**40,050**	7,912	6,004	8,454	6,794
40,050	**40,100**	7,926	6,011	8,468	6,808
40,100	**40,150**	7,940	6,019	8,482	6,822
40,150	**40,200**	7,954	6,026	8,496	6,836
40,200	**40,250**	7,968	6,034	8,510	6,850
40,250	**40,300**	7,982	6,041	8,524	6,864
40,300	**40,350**	7,996	6,049	8,538	6,878
40,350	**40,400**	8,010	6,056	8,552	6,892
40,400	**40,450**	8,024	6,064	8,566	6,906
40,450	**40,500**	8,038	6,071	8,580	6,920
40,500	**40,550**	8,052	6,079	8,594	6,934
40,550	**40,600**	8,066	6,086	8,608	6,948
40,600	**40,650**	8,080	6,094	8,622	6,962
40,650	**40,700**	8,094	6,101	8,636	6,976
40,700	**40,750**	8,108	6,109	8,650	6,990
40,750	**40,800**	8,122	6,116	8,664	7,004
40,800	**40,850**	8,136	6,124	8,678	7,018
40,850	**40,900**	8,150	6,131	8,692	7,032
40,900	**40,950**	8,164	6,139	8,706	7,046
40,950	**41,000**	8,178	6,146	8,720	7,060

* This column must also be used by a qualifying widow(er).

Continued on next page

1998 Tax Table—*Continued*

41,000

If Form 1040A, line 24, is— At least	But less than	And you are— Single	Married filing jointly *	Married filing separately	Head of a household
		Your tax is—			
41,000	**41,050**	8,192	6,154	8,734	7,074
41,050	**41,100**	8,206	6,161	8,748	7,088
41,100	**41,150**	8,220	6,169	8,762	7,102
41,150	**41,200**	8,234	6,176	8,776	7,116
41,200	**41,250**	8,248	6,184	8,790	7,130
41,250	**41,300**	8,262	6,191	8,804	7,144
41,300	**41,350**	8,276	6,199	8,818	7,158
41,350	**41,400**	8,290	6,206	8,832	7,172
41,400	**41,450**	8,304	6,214	8,846	7,186
41,450	**41,500**	8,318	6,221	8,860	7,200
41,500	**41,550**	8,332	6,229	8,874	7,214
41,550	**41,600**	8,346	6,236	8,888	7,228
41,600	**41,650**	8,360	6,244	8,902	7,242
41,650	**41,700**	8,374	6,251	8,916	7,256
41,700	**41,750**	8,388	6,259	8,930	7,270
41,750	**41,800**	8,402	6,266	8,944	7,284
41,800	**41,850**	8,416	6,274	8,958	7,298
41,850	**41,900**	8,430	6,281	8,972	7,312
41,900	**41,950**	8,444	6,289	8,986	7,326
41,950	**42,000**	8,458	6,296	9,000	7,340

42,000

At least	But less than	Single	Married filing jointly *	Married filing separately	Head of a household
42,000	**42,050**	8,472	6,304	9,014	7,354
42,050	**42,100**	8,486	6,311	9,028	7,368
42,100	**42,150**	8,500	6,319	9,042	7,382
42,150	**42,200**	8,514	6,326	9,056	7,396
42,200	**42,250**	8,528	6,334	9,070	7,410
42,250	**42,300**	8,542	6,341	9,084	7,424
42,300	**42,350**	8,556	6,349	9,098	7,438
42,350	**42,400**	8,570	6,360	9,112	7,452
42,400	**42,450**	8,584	6,374	9,126	7,466
42,450	**42,500**	8,598	6,388	9,140	7,480
42,500	**42,550**	8,612	6,402	9,154	7,494
42,550	**42,600**	8,626	6,416	9,168	7,508
42,600	**42,650**	8,640	6,430	9,182	7,522
42,650	**42,700**	8,654	6,444	9,196	7,536
42,700	**42,750**	8,668	6,458	9,210	7,550
42,750	**42,800**	8,682	6,472	9,224	7,564
42,800	**42,850**	8,696	6,486	9,238	7,578
42,850	**42,900**	8,710	6,500	9,252	7,592
42,900	**42,950**	8,724	6,514	9,266	7,606
42,950	**43,000**	8,738	6,528	9,280	7,620

43,000

At least	But less than	Single	Married filing jointly *	Married filing separately	Head of a household
43,000	**43,050**	8,752	6,542	9,294	7,634
43,050	**43,100**	8,766	6,556	9,308	7,648
43,100	**43,150**	8,780	6,570	9,322	7,662
43,150	**43,200**	8,794	6,584	9,336	7,676
43,200	**43,250**	8,808	6,598	9,350	7,690
43,250	**43,300**	8,822	6,612	9,364	7,704
43,300	**43,350**	8,836	6,626	9,378	7,718
43,350	**43,400**	8,850	6,640	9,392	7,732
43,400	**43,450**	8,864	6,654	9,406	7,746
43,450	**43,500**	8,878	6,668	9,420	7,760
43,500	**43,550**	8,892	6,682	9,434	7,774
43,550	**43,600**	8,906	6,696	9,448	7,788
43,600	**43,650**	8,920	6,710	[illegible]	[illegible]
43,650	**43,700**	8,934	6,724	9,476	7,816
43,700	**43,750**	8,948	6,738	9,490	7,830
43,750	**43,800**	8,962	6,752	9,504	7,844
43,800	**43,850**	8,976	6,766	9,518	7,858
43,850	**43,900**	8,990	6,780	9,532	7,872
43,900	**43,950**	9,004	6,794	9,546	7,886
43,950	**44,000**	9,018	6,808	9,560	7,900

44,000

At least	But less than	Single	Married filing jointly *	Married filing separately	Head of a household
44,000	**44,050**	9,032	6,822	9,574	7,914
44,050	**44,100**	9,046	6,836	9,588	7,928
44,100	**44,150**	9,060	6,850	9,602	7,942
44,150	**44,200**	9,074	6,864	9,616	7,956
44,200	**44,250**	9,088	6,878	9,630	7,970
44,250	**44,300**	9,102	6,892	9,644	7,984
44,300	**44,350**	9,116	6,906	9,658	7,998
44,350	**44,400**	9,130	6,920	9,672	8,012
44,400	**44,450**	9,144	6,934	9,686	8,026
44,450	**44,500**	9,158	6,948	9,700	8,040
44,500	**44,550**	9,172	6,962	9,714	8,054
44,550	**44,600**	9,186	6,976	9,728	8,068
44,600	**44,650**	9,200	6,990	9,742	8,082
44,650	**44,700**	9,214	7,004	9,756	8,096
44,700	**44,750**	9,228	7,018	9,770	8,110
44,750	**44,800**	9,242	7,032	9,784	8,124
44,800	**44,850**	9,256	7,046	9,798	8,138
44,850	**44,900**	9,270	7,060	9,812	8,152
44,900	**44,950**	9,284	7,074	9,826	8,166
44,950	**45,000**	9,298	7,088	9,840	8,180

45,000

At least	But less than	Single	Married filing jointly *	Married filing separately	Head of a household
45,000	**45,050**	9,312	7,102	9,854	8,194
45,050	**45,100**	9,326	7,116	9,868	8,208
45,100	**45,150**	9,340	7,130	9,882	8,222
45,150	**45,200**	9,354	7,144	9,896	8,236
45,200	**45,250**	9,368	7,158	9,910	8,250
45,250	**45,300**	9,382	7,172	9,924	8,264
45,300	**45,350**	9,396	7,186	9,938	8,278
45,350	**45,400**	9,410	7,200	9,952	8,292
45,400	**45,450**	9,424	7,214	9,966	8,306
45,450	**45,500**	9,438	7,228	9,980	8,320
45,500	**45,550**	9,452	7,242	9,994	8,334
45,550	**45,600**	9,466	7,256	10,008	8,348
45,600	**45,650**	9,480	7,270	10,022	8,362
45,650	**45,700**	9,494	7,284	10,036	8,376
45,700	**45,750**	9,508	7,298	10,050	8,390
45,750	**45,800**	9,522	7,312	10,064	8,404
45,800	**45,850**	9,536	7,326	10,078	8,418
45,850	**45,900**	9,550	7,340	10,092	8,432
45,900	**45,950**	9,564	7,354	10,106	8,446
45,950	**46,000**	9,578	7,368	10,120	8,460

46,000

At least	But less than	Single	Married filing jointly *	Married filing separately	Head of a household
46,000	**46,050**	9,592	7,382	10,134	8,474
46,050	**46,100**	9,606	7,396	10,148	8,488
46,100	**46,150**	9,620	7,410	10,162	8,502
46,150	**46,200**	9,634	7,424	10,176	8,516
46,200	**46,250**	9,648	7,438	10,190	8,530
46,250	**46,300**	9,662	7,452	10,204	8,544
46,300	**46,350**	9,676	7,466	10,218	8,558
46,350	**46,400**	9,690	7,480	10,232	8,572
46,400	**46,450**	9,704	7,494	10,246	8,586
46,450	**46,500**	9,718	7,508	10,260	8,600
46,500	**46,550**	9,732	7,522	10,274	8,614
46,550	**46,600**	9,746	7,536	10,288	8,628
[illegible]	**[illegible]**	9,760	7,550	10,302	8,642
46,650	**46,700**	9,774	7,564	10,316	8,656
46,700	**46,750**	9,788	7,578	10,330	8,670
46,750	**46,800**	9,802	7,592	10,344	8,684
46,800	**46,850**	9,816	7,606	10,358	8,698
46,850	**46,900**	9,830	7,620	10,372	8,712
46,900	**46,950**	9,844	7,634	10,386	8,726
46,950	**47,000**	9,858	7,648	10,400	8,740

47,000

At least	But less than	Single	Married filing jointly *	Married filing separately	Head of a household
47,000	**47,050**	9,872	7,662	10,414	8,754
47,050	**47,100**	9,886	7,676	10,428	8,768
47,100	**47,150**	9,900	7,690	10,442	8,782
47,150	**47,200**	9,914	7,704	10,456	8,796
47,200	**47,250**	9,928	7,718	10,470	8,810
47,250	**47,300**	9,942	7,732	10,484	8,824
47,300	**47,350**	9,956	7,746	10,498	8,838
47,350	**47,400**	9,970	7,760	10,512	8,852
47,400	**47,450**	9,984	7,774	10,526	8,866
47,450	**47,500**	9,998	7,788	10,540	8,880
47,500	**47,550**	10,012	7,802	10,554	8,894
47,550	**47,600**	10,026	7,816	10,568	8,908
47,600	**47,650**	10,040	7,830	10,582	8,922
47,650	**47,700**	10,054	7,844	10,596	8,936
47,700	**47,750**	10,068	7,858	10,610	8,950
47,750	**47,800**	10,082	7,872	10,624	8,964
47,800	**47,850**	10,096	7,886	10,638	8,978
47,850	**47,900**	10,110	7,900	10,652	8,992
47,900	**47,950**	10,124	7,914	10,666	9,006
47,950	**48,000**	10,138	7,928	10,680	9,020

48,000

At least	But less than	Single	Married filing jointly *	Married filing separately	Head of a household
48,000	**48,050**	10,152	7,942	10,694	9,034
48,050	**48,100**	10,166	7,956	10,708	9,048
48,100	**48,150**	10,180	7,970	10,722	9,062
48,150	**48,200**	10,194	7,984	10,736	9,076
48,200	**48,250**	10,208	7,998	10,750	9,090
48,250	**48,300**	10,222	8,012	10,764	9,104
48,300	**48,350**	10,236	8,026	10,778	9,118
48,350	**48,400**	10,250	8,040	10,792	9,132
48,400	**48,450**	10,264	8,054	10,806	9,146
48,450	**48,500**	10,278	8,068	10,820	9,160
48,500	**48,550**	10,292	8,082	10,834	9,174
48,550	**48,600**	10,306	8,096	10,848	9,188
48,600	**48,650**	10,320	8,110	10,862	9,202
48,650	**48,700**	10,334	8,124	10,876	9,216
48,700	**48,750**	10,348	8,138	10,890	9,230
48,750	**48,800**	10,362	8,152	10,904	9,244
48,800	**48,850**	10,376	8,166	10,918	9,258
48,850	**48,900**	10,390	8,180	10,932	9,272
48,900	**48,950**	10,404	8,194	10,946	9,286
48,950	**49,000**	10,418	8,208	10,960	9,300

49,000

At least	But less than	Single	Married filing jointly *	Married filing separately	Head of a household
49,000	**49,050**	10,432	8,222	10,974	9,314
49,050	**49,100**	10,446	8,236	10,988	9,328
49,100	**49,150**	10,460	8,250	11,002	9,342
49,150	**49,200**	10,474	8,264	11,016	9,356
49,200	**49,250**	10,488	8,278	11,030	9,370
49,250	**49,300**	10,502	8,292	11,044	9,384
49,300	**49,350**	10,516	8,306	11,058	9,398
49,350	**49,400**	10,530	8,320	11,072	9,412
49,400	**49,450**	10,544	8,334	11,086	9,426
49,450	**49,500**	10,558	8,348	11,100	9,440
49,500	**49,550**	10,572	8,362	11,114	9,454
49,550	**49,600**	10,586	8,376	11,128	9,468
49,600	**49,650**	10,600	8,390	11,142	9,482
49,650	**49,700**	10,614	8,404	11,156	9,496
49,700	**49,750**	10,628	8,418	11,170	9,510
49,750	**49,800**	10,642	8,432	11,184	9,524
49,800	**49,850**	10,656	8,446	11,198	9,538
49,850	**49,900**	10,670	8,460	11,212	9,552
49,900	**49,950**	10,684	8,474	11,226	9,566
49,950	**50,000**	10,698	8,488	11,240	9,580

* This column must also be used by a qualifying widow(er).

50,000 or over— use Form 1040

Appendix

In this section you will practice filling out:

- Schedule 1
- Schedule 2
- Schedule EIC (earned income credit)

SCHEDULE 1

Schedule 1 is for taxpayers of any age who:

- had over $400 in taxable interest income

OR

- had Series EE U.S. savings bonds and are claiming the exclusion of interest for these savings

OR

- had over $400 in dividends.

On the top line of this form, print your first and last name. Also write your Social Security number.

Part I

1. List the names of all of the banks that paid you interest. Fill in the amount of interest you received from each bank.
2. Add all of the amounts listed in 1. Write the total on line 2.
3. Total the amount of excludable interest you received on your savings bonds Series EE.
4. Subtract line 3 from line 2 (line 3 – line 2). Write this amount on this form, line 4, and on Form 1040A, line 8a.

Part II

5. List the names of all of the companies that paid you dividends on their stocks or bonds. Also fill in the amount of dividends you received from each company.
6. Add all of the amounts listed in 5. Write this amount on this form, line 6, and on Form 1040A, line 9.

SCHEDULE 1—SIDE 1

Schedule 1 (Form 1040A)

Department of the Treasury—Internal Revenue Service

Interest and Ordinary Dividends for Form 1040A Filers

1998

OMB No. 1545-0085

Name(s) shown on Form 1040A | **Your social security number**

Part I

Interest

(See pages 24 and 56.)

Note: *If you received a Form 1099–INT, Form 1099–OID, or substitute statement from a brokerage firm, enter the firm's name and the total interest shown on that form.*

			Amount
1	List name of payer. If any interest is from a seller-financed mortgage and the buyer used the property as a personal residence, see page 56 and list this interest first. Also, show that buyer's social security number and address.	1	
2	Add the amounts on line 1.	2	
3	Excludable interest on series EE U.S. savings bonds issued after 1989 from Form 8815, line 14. You **must** attach Form 8815 to Form 1040A.	3	
4	Subtract line 3 from line 2. Enter the result here and on Form 1040A, line 8a.	4	

Part II

Ordinary dividends

(See pages 24 and 56.)

Note: *If you received a Form 1099–DIV or substitute statement from a brokerage firm, enter the firm's name and the ordinary dividends shown on that form.*

			Amount
5	List name of payer	5	
6	Add the amounts on line 5. Enter the total here and on Form 1040A, line 9.	6	

For Paperwork Reduction Act Notice, see Form 1040A instructions. Cat. No. 12075R **1998 Schedule 1 (Form 1040A)**

SCHEDULE 2

Schedule 2 is for taxpayers who:

- paid for the care of one or more qualifying persons

AND

- lived with the qualifying person or persons

AND

- earned income during the year

AND

- paid for the care in order to be able to work or look for a job

AND

- are not using the filing status of married couple, filing separately.

A qualifying person is:

- your dependent who was under the age of 13 when the care was provided and for whom you claim an exemption on Form 1040A

OR

- your spouse who was physically or mentally unable to care for himself/herself

OR

- your dependent who was unable to care for himself/herself and for whom you claim an exemption on Form 1040A.

If you paid child or dependent care expenses for at least one qualifying person, you should complete Schedule 2.

On the top line of this form, print your first and last name. Also write your Social Security number.

In Part 1, you will need to provide information about the people or organizations that provided the child or dependent care.

Part I 1a. Print the name of each provider.

1b. Print the address of each provider.

1c. Write the Social Security number or Employer Identification number of each provider.

1d. Write the total amount paid to each provider.

If you received employer-provided dependent care benefits, complete Part III.

If you did not receive employer-provided dependent care benefits, complete only Part II.

Part II 2a. Print the first and last name of each qualifying person.

2b. Print the Social Security number of each qualifying person.

2c. Print the amount of expenses you paid for each qualifying person.

3. Add the amounts listed in 2c. Do not write more than $2,400 for one qualifying person or $4,800 for two or more persons.

4. Write the amount of your earned income (from your W-2 form(s)).

5. If you are married and filing a joint return, write the amount of your spouse's earned income. Otherwise, write your earned income from line 4.

6. Compare the amounts on lines 3, 4, and 5. Write the smallest of the three amounts on line 6.

7. Write the amount from Form 1040A, line 19 on line 7 of Schedule 2.

8. Find the decimal amount that applies to the amount on line 7.

9. Multiply the amount on line 6 by the decimal amount on line 8. Write the result on line 9.

Write the amount on line 9 also on Form 1040A, line 26.

1040A AND SCHEDULE 2

Activity: Fill out forms for Margaret Murphy.

Margaret Murphy is a computer programmer. She is single and she earned $26,500. She did not earn any interest during the year, and her itemized deductions were less than $500. She had $2,860 of federal income tax withheld from her pay. She has a daughter Colleen, who is eight years old. She paid the YMCA to care for her daughter. Her child-care expenses for the year totaled $3,000.

She lives at 418 Main Street, Westwyck, Massachusetts 05000. She wants to contribute to the Presidential Campaign Election fund.

The EIN of the YMCA is 94-1654052. Its address is 615 49th Street, Westwyck, Massachusetts 05000.

Margaret's Social Security number is 600-55-4213. Colleen's Social Security number is 600-33-3124.

W-2—MARGARET MURPHY

a Control number	OMB No. 1545-0008	
b Employer identification number 9516464464	**1** Wages, tips, other compensation 26,500.00	**2** Federal income tax withheld 2,860.00
c Employer's name, address, and ZIP code Superior Computer Services 14 Gates Avenue Suite 301 Westwyck, MA 05000	**3** Social security wages 26,500.00	**4** Social security tax withheld 1,643.00
	5 Medicare wages and tips 26,500.00	**6** Medicare tax withheld 384.25
	7 Social security tips	**8** Allocated tips
d Employee's social security number 600-55-4213	**9** Advance EIC payment	**10** Dependent care benefits
e Employee's name (first, middle initial, last) Margaret Murphy 418 Main Street Westwyck, MA 05000	**11** Nonqualified plans	**12** Benefits included in box 1
	13 See instrs. for box 13	**14** Other
f Employee's address and ZIP code	**15** Statutory employee ☐ Deceased ☐ Pension plan ☐ Legal rep. ☐ Deferred compensation ☐	

16 State	Employer's state I.D. no.	**17** State wages, tips, etc.	**18** State income tax	**19** Locality name	**20** Local wages, tips, etc.	**21** Local income tax
MA		26,500.00	250.00			

1040A—PAGE 1

Form **1040A** Department of the Treasury–Internal Revenue Service
U.S. Individual Income Tax Return **1998** IRS Use Only–Do not write or staple in this space.

OMB No. 1545-0085

Label (See page 18.)

Use the IRS label. Otherwise, please print or type.

LABEL HERE

Your first name and initial	Last name		**Your social security number**
If a joint return, spouse's first name and initial	Last name		**Spouse's social security number**
Home address (number and street). If you have a P.O. box, see page 19.		Apt. no.	
City, town or post office, state, and ZIP code. If you have a foreign address, see page 19.			

▲ IMPORTANT! ▲ You **must** enter your SSN(s) above.

Presidential Election Campaign Fund (See page 19.)

	Yes	No
Do you want $3 to go to this fund?		
If a joint return, does your spouse want $3 to go to this fund?		

Note: *Checking "Yes" will not change your tax or reduce your refund.*

Filing status

Check only one box.

1 ☐ Single
2 ☐ Married filing joint return (even if only one had income)
3 ☐ Married filing separate return. Enter spouse's social security number above and full name here. ▶ ________
4 ☐ Head of household (with qualifying person). (See page 20.) If the qualifying person is a child but not your dependent, enter this child's name here. ▶ ________
5 ☐ Qualifying widow(er) with dependent child (year spouse died ▶ 19   ). (See page 21.)

Exemptions

6a ☐ **Yourself.** If your parent (or someone else) can claim you as a dependent on his or her tax return, **do not** check box 6a.
b ☐ **Spouse**

No. of boxes checked on 6a and 6b ____

c **Dependents:**

If more than seven dependents, see page 21.

(1) First name Last name	(2) Dependent's social security number	(3) Dependent's relationship to you	(4) ✓ if qualified child for child tax credit (see page 22)
			☐
			☐
			☐
			☐
			☐
			☐
			☐

No. of your children on 6c who:
• lived with you ____
• did not live with you due to divorce or separation (see page 23) ____
Dependents on 6c not entered above ____

d Total number of exemptions claimed.

Add numbers entered on lines above ☐

Income

Attach Copy B of your Forms W-2 and 1099-R here.

If you did not get a W-2, see page 24.

Enclose, but do not staple, any payment.

7	Wages, salaries, tips, etc. Attach Form(s) W-2.		7
8a	**Taxable** interest. Attach Schedule 1 if required.		8a
b	**Tax-exempt** interest. DO NOT include on line 8a.	8b	
9	Ordinary dividends. Attach Schedule 1 if required.		9
10a	Total IRA distributions. 10a	**10b** Taxable amount (see page 24).	10b
11a	Total pensions and annuities. 11a	**11b** Taxable amount (see page 25).	11b
12	Unemployment compensation.		12
13a	Social security benefits. 13a	**13b** Taxable amount (see page 27).	13b
14	Add lines 7 through 13b (far right column). This is your **total income.** ▶		14

Adjusted gross income

15	IRA deduction (see page 28).	15	
16	Student loan interest deduction (see page 28).	16	
17	Add lines 15 and 16. These are your **total adjustments.**		17
18	Subtract line 17 from line 14. This is your **adjusted gross income.** If under $30,095 (under $10,030 if a child did not live with you), see the EIC instructions on page 36. ▶		18

For Disclosure, Privacy Act, and Paperwork Reduction Act Notice, see page 49. Cat. No. 11327A **1998 Form 1040A**

1040A—PAGE 2

1998 Form 1040A page 2

Taxable income

19 Enter the amount from line 18. 19

20a Check if: ☐ **You** were 65 or older ☐ Blind ☐ **Spouse** was 65 or older ☐ Blind **Enter number of boxes checked** ▶ 20a ☐

b If you are married filing separately and your spouse itemizes deductions, see page 30 and check here . . . . . . ▶ 20b ☐

21 Enter the **standard deduction** for your filing status. **But** see page 31 if you checked any box on line 20a or 20b **OR** if someone can claim you as a dependent.
- Single—$4,250
- Married filing jointly or Qualifying widow(er)—$7,100
- Head of household—$6,250
- Married filing separately—$3,550 21

22 Subtract line 21 from line 19. If line 21 is more than line 19, enter -0-. 22

23 Multiply $2,700 by the total number of exemptions claimed on line 6d. 23

24 Subtract line 23 from line 22. If line 23 is more than line 22, enter -0-. This is your **taxable income.** ▶ 24

Tax, credits, and payments

25 Find the tax on the amount on line 24 (see page 31). 25

26 Credit for child and dependent care expenses. Attach Schedule 2. 26

27 Credit for the elderly or the disabled. Attach Schedule 3. 27

28 Child tax credit (see page 32). 28

29 Education credits. Attach Form 8863. 29

30 Adoption credit. Attach Form 8839. 30

31 Add lines 26 through 30. These are your **total credits.** 31

32 Subtract line 31 from line 25. If line 31 is more than line 25, enter -0-. 32

33 Advance earned income credit payments from Form(s) W-2. 33

34 Add lines 32 and 33. This is your **total tax.** ▶ 34

35 Total Federal income tax withheld from Forms W-2 and 1099. 35

36 1998 estimated tax payments and amount applied from 1997 return. 36

37a **Earned income credit.** Attach Schedule EIC if you have a qualifying child. 37a

b Nontaxable earned income: amount ▶ and type ▶

38 Additional child tax credit. Attach Form 8812. 38

39 Add lines 35, 36, 37a, and 38. These are your **total payments.** ▶ 39

Refund

Have it directly deposited! See page 43 and fill in 41b, 41c, and 41d.

40 If line 39 is more than line 34, subtract line 34 from line 39. This is the amount you **overpaid.** 40

41a Amount of line 40 you want **refunded to you.** 41a

b Routing number ☐☐☐☐☐☐☐☐☐ c Type: ☐ Checking ☐ Savings

d Account number ☐☐☐☐☐☐☐☐☐☐☐☐☐☐☐☐☐

42 Amount of line 40 you want **applied to your 1999 estimated tax.** 42

Amount you owe

43 If line 34 is more than line 39, subtract line 39 from line 34. This is the **amount you owe.** For details on how to pay, see page 44. 43

44 Estimated tax penalty (see page 44). 44

Sign here

Joint return? See page 19. Keep a copy for your records.

Under penalties of perjury, I declare that I have examined this return and accompanying schedules and statements, and to the best of my knowledge and belief, they are true, correct, and accurately list all amounts and sources of income I received during the tax year. Declaration of preparer (other than the taxpayer) is based on all information of which the preparer has any knowledge.

Your signature	Date	Your occupation	Daytime telephone number (optional)
Spouse's signature. If joint return, BOTH must sign.	Date	Spouse's occupation	( )

Paid preparer's use only

Preparer's signature ▶	Date	Check if self-employed ☐	Preparer's social security no.
Firm's name (or yours if self-employed) and address ▶			EIN
			ZIP code

SCHEDULE 2—PAGE 1

Schedule 2 (Form 1040A) — Department of the Treasury—Internal Revenue Service

Child and Dependent Care Expenses for Form 1040A Filers (99) 1998

OMB No. 1545-0085

Name(s) shown on Form 1040A | **Your social security number**

Before you begin, you need to understand the following terms. See **Definitions** on page 57.
- **Dependent Care Benefits**
- **Qualifying Person(s)**
- **Qualified Expenses**
- **Earned Income**

Part I — Persons or organizations who provided the care

You MUST complete this part.

1 **(a)** Care provider's name	**(b)** Address (number, street, apt. no., city, state, and ZIP code)	**(c)** Identifying number (SSN or EIN)	**(d)** Amount paid (see page 58)

(If you need more space, use the bottom of page 2.)

Did you receive **dependent care benefits?**
- **No** → Complete only Part II below.
- **Yes** → Complete Part III on the back next.

Caution: *If the care was provided in your home, you may owe employment taxes. If you do, you must use Form 1040. See* ***Schedule H*** *and its instructions for details.*

Part II — Credit for child and dependent care expenses

2 Information about your **qualifying person(s).** If you have more than two qualifying persons, see page 58.

(a) Qualifying person's name — First	Last	**(b)** Qualifying person's social security number	**(c) Qualified expenses** you incurred and paid in 1998 for the person listed in column (a)

3 Add the amounts in column (c) of line 2. DO NOT enter more than $2,400 for one qualifying person or $4,800 for two or more persons. If you completed Part III, enter the amount from line 24. — 3

4 Enter YOUR **earned income.** — 4

5 If married filing a joint return, enter YOUR SPOUSE'S earned income (if your spouse was a student or was disabled, see page 59); **all others,** enter the amount from line 4. — 5

6 Enter the **smallest** of line 3, 4, or 5. — 6

7 Enter the amount from Form 1040A, line 19. — 7

8 Enter on line 8 the decimal amount shown below that applies to the amount on line 7.

If line 7 is— Over — But not over	**Decimal amount is**	**If line 7 is— Over — But not over**	**Decimal amount is**
$0—10,000	.30	$20,000—22,000	.24
10,000—12,000	.29	22,000—24,000	.23
12,000—14,000	.28	24,000—26,000	.22
14,000—16,000	.27	26,000—28,000	.21
16,000—18,000	.26	28,000—No limit	.20
18,000—20,000	.25		

8 .

9 Multiply **line 6** by the decimal amount on line 8. Enter the result. Then, see page 59 for the amount of credit to enter on Form 1040A, line 26. — 9

For Paperwork Reduction Act Notice, see Form 1040A instructions. Cat. No. 10749I **1998 Schedule 2 (Form 1040A)**

SCHEDULE 2—PAGE 2

1998 Schedule 2 (Form 1040A) page 2

Part III

Dependent care benefits

10	Enter the total amount of **dependent care benefits** you received for 1998. This amount should be shown in box 10 of your W-2 form(s). DO NOT include amounts that were reported to you as wages in box 1 of Form(s) W-2.			10
11	Enter the amount forfeited, if any. See page 59.			11
12	Subtract line 11 from line 10.			12
13	Enter the total amount of **qualified expenses** incurred in 1998 for the care of the qualifying person(s).	13		
14	Enter the **smaller** of line 12 or 13.	14		
15	Enter YOUR **earned income.**	15		
16	If married filing a joint return, enter YOUR SPOUSE'S earned income (if your spouse was a student or was disabled, see the instructions for line 5); if married filing a separate return, see the instructions for the amount to enter; **all others,** enter the amount from line 15.	16		
17	Enter the **smallest** of line 14, 15, or 16.	17		
18	**Excluded benefits.** Enter here the **smaller** of the following: • The amount from line 17, or • $5,000 ($2,500 if married filing a separate return **and** you were required to enter your spouse's earned income on line 16).			18
19	**Taxable benefits.** Subtract line 18 from line 12. Also, include this amount on Form 1040A, line 7. In the space to the left of line 7, enter "DCB."			19

To claim the child and dependent care credit, complete lines 20–24 below.

20	Enter $2,400 ($4,800 if two or more qualifying persons).	20	
21	Enter the amount from line 18.	21	
22	Subtract line 21 from line 20. If zero or less, **STOP.** You cannot take the credit. **Exception.** If you paid 1997 expenses in 1998, see the instructions for line 9.	22	
23	Complete line 2 on the front of this schedule. DO NOT include in column (c) any excluded benefits shown on line 18 above. Then, add the amounts in column (c) and enter the total here.	23	
24	Enter the **smaller** of line 22 or 23 here. Also, enter this amount on line 3 on the front of this schedule and complete lines 4–9.	24	

1040A—CHILD TAX CREDIT WORKSHEET

Child Tax Credit Worksheet–Line 28

▶ Keep for your records.

Do Not File

1. $400.00 × ________ . Multiply and enter the result . . . . 1. ________
Enter number of qualifying children (see page 32)

2. Enter the amount from Form 1040A, line 19 . . . . . . 2. ________

3. Is line 2 above more than $55,000?

☐ **No.** Skip lines 3 through 5, enter -0- on line 6, and go to line 7.

☐ **Yes.** Enter: $75,000 if single, head of household, or qualifying widow(er); $110,000 if married filing jointly; $55,000 if married filing separately . . . . . . 3. ________

4. Subtract line 3 from line 2. If zero or less, enter -0- here and on line 6, and go to line 7 . . . . 4. ________

5. Divide line 4 by $1,000. If the result is not a whole number, round it up to the next higher whole number (for example, round 0.01 to 1) . . . . 5. ________

6. Multiply $50 by the number on line 5 . . . . 6. ________

7. Subtract line 6 from line 1. If zero or less, **stop here;** you **cannot** take this credit . 7. ________

8. Enter the amount from Form 1040A, line 25 . . . . . . 8. ________

9. Is line 1 above more than $800?

☐ **No.** Add the amounts from Form 1040A, lines 26, 27, and 29. Enter the total.

☐ **Yes.** Enter the amount from the worksheet on page 34. } 9. ________

10. Subtract line 9 above from line 8 . . . . 10. ________

11. **Child tax credit.** Enter the **smaller** of line 7 or line 10 here and on Form 1040A, line 28 ▶ 11. ________

TIP *If line 1 above is more than $800, you may be able to take the* ***Additional Child Tax Credit.*** *See page 32.*

SCHEDULE EIC

Schedule EIC (earned income credit) is for a taxpayer of any age who:

- worked and earned less than $30,095

AND

- completed Form 1040A, indicating that line 8 was less than $30,095

AND

- is not using the filing status of married couple, filing separately

AND

- has at least one qualifying child

AND

- is not a qualifying child himself/herself.

A "qualifying child" is your:

☐ son

☐ daughter

☐ adopted child

☐ grandchild

☐ stepchild

☐ foster child

- who was under the age of 19

OR

- under the age of 24 and a full-time student

OR

- any age and permanently and totally disabled

AND

- who lived with you in the United States for more than six months (or all year if a foster child).

If you have at least one qualifying child, and fulfill all of the requirements listed before, you may complete Schedule EIC.

On the top line of this form, print your first and last name. Also write your Social Security number.

You will need to provide information about a maximum of two qualifying children.

1. Print each child's first name and last name.
2. Write each child's year of birth.

3a. For a child born before 1980, check if the child was a student under the age of 24.

3b. For a child born before 1980, check if the child was disabled.

4. Write the child's Social Security number.
5. Indicate the child's relationship to you.
6. Indicate the number of months the child lived with you in the United States.

If you want the IRS to calculate your credit for you, write "EIC" next to line 37a of Form 1040A.

If you want to calculate your credit yourself, you will need to fill out the worksheet provided with the 1040A instructions.

1040A AND EIC PRACTICE

Activity: Fill out the forms for Jamal Answar and his family.

Jamal Answar earned $18,000 as a factory worker, and his wife, Radira, stayed home to care for the children. Their son, Jumur, is two years old. Their daughter, Lale, is one year old.

They have no savings account and $1,000 in deductions. Jamal had $400 withheld from his pay.

They are eligible to receive the earned income credit (EIC). They do not have health insurance.

Jamal and Radira live at 257 8th Street, Apt. 110, Atlanta, Georgia 30000. They want to contribute to the Presidential Election Campaign fund. The Social Security numbers for the family are:

Jamal:	008-54-1482
Radira:	008-07-8304
Jumur:	008-71-3418
Lale:	008-33-2596

W-2—JAMAL ANSWAR

a Control number	22222	Void ☐	For Official Use Only ►

b Employer identification number 9514545454	1 Wages, tips, other compensation 18,000.00	2 Federal income tax withheld 400.00
c Employer's name, address, and ZIP code Consolidated Electronics, Inc. 965 Edison Drive Atlanta, GA 30000	3 Social security wages 18,000.00	4 Social security tax withheld 1,116.00
	5 Medicare wages and tips 18,000.00	6 Medicare tax withheld 261.00
	7 Social security tips	8 Allocated tips
d Employee's social security number 008-54-1482	9 Advance EIC payment	10 Dependent care benefits
e Employee's name (first, middle initial, last) Jamal Answar	11 Nonqualified plans	12 Benefits included in box 1
257 8th Street APT 110 Atlanta, GA 30000	13 See instrs. for box 13	14 Other
f Employee's address and ZIP code	15 Statutory employee ☐ Deceased ☐ Pension plan ☐ Legal rep. ☐ Deferred compensation ☐	

16 State	Employer's state I.D. no.	17 State wages, tips, etc.	18 State income tax	19 Locality name	20 Local wages, tips, etc.	21 Local income tax
GA		18,000.00	100.00			

1040A—PAGE 1

Form **1040A** | Department of the Treasury–Internal Revenue Service | **U.S. Individual Income Tax Return** | **1998** | IRS Use Only–Do not write or staple in this space.

OMB No. 1545-0085

Label
(See page 18.)

Use the IRS label. Otherwise, please print or type.

LABEL HERE

Your first name and initial	Last name	**Your social security number**
If a joint return, spouse's first name and initial	Last name	**Spouse's social security number**
Home address (number and street). If you have a P.O. box, see page 19.	Apt. no.	
City, town or post office, state, and ZIP code. If you have a foreign address, see page 19.		

▲ IMPORTANT! ▲
You **must** enter your SSN(s) above.

Presidential Election Campaign Fund (See page 19.)

	Yes	No
Do you want $3 to go to this fund?		
If a joint return, does your spouse want $3 to go to this fund?		

Note: *Checking "Yes" will not change your tax or reduce your refund.*

Filing status

Check only one box.

1 ☐ Single
2 ☐ Married filing joint return (even if only one had income)
3 ☐ Married filing separate return. Enter spouse's social security number above and full name here. ▶
4 ☐ Head of household (with qualifying person). (See page 20.) If the qualifying person is a child but not your dependent, enter this child's name here. ▶
5 ☐ Qualifying widow(er) with dependent child (year spouse died ▶ 19). (See page 21.)

Exemptions

6a ☐ **Yourself.** If your parent (or someone else) can claim you as a dependent on his or her tax return, **do not** check box 6a.
b ☐ **Spouse**

No. of boxes checked on 6a and 6b ____

c **Dependents:**

If more than seven dependents, see page 21.

(1) First name Last name	(2) Dependent's social security number	(3) Dependent's relationship to you	(4) ✓ if qualified child for child tax credit (see page 22)
			☐
			☐
			☐
			☐
			☐
			☐
			☐

No. of your children on 6c who:
- **lived with you** ____
- **did not live with you due to divorce or separation (see page 23)** ____

Dependents on 6c not entered above ____

d Total number of exemptions claimed.

Add numbers entered on lines above ☐

Income

Attach Copy B of your Forms W-2 and 1099-R here.

If you did not get a W-2, see page 24.

Enclose, but do not staple, any payment.

Line	Description		
7	Wages, salaries, tips, etc. Attach Form(s) W-2.		7
8a	**Taxable** interest. Attach Schedule 1 if required.		8a
b	**Tax-exempt** interest. DO NOT include on line 8a.	8b	
9	Ordinary dividends. Attach Schedule 1 if required.		9
10a	Total IRA distributions. 10a	**10b** Taxable amount (see page 24).	10b
11a	Total pensions and annuities. 11a	**11b** Taxable amount (see page 25).	11b
12	Unemployment compensation.		12
13a	Social security benefits. 13a	**13b** Taxable amount (see page 27).	13b
14	Add lines 7 through 13b (far right column). This is your **total income.** ▶		14

Adjusted gross income

Line	Description		
15	IRA deduction (see page 28).	15	
16	Student loan interest deduction (see page 28).	16	
17	Add lines 15 and 16. These are your **total adjustments.**		17
18	Subtract line 17 from line 14. This is your **adjusted gross income.** If under $30,095 (under $10,030 if a child did not live with you), see the EIC instructions on page 36. ▶		18

For Disclosure, Privacy Act, and Paperwork Reduction Act Notice, see page 49. Cat. No. 11327A **1998 Form 1040A**

1040A—PAGE 2

1998 Form 1040A page 2

Taxable income

19 Enter the amount from line 18. 19

20a Check if: ☐ **You** were 65 or older ☐ Blind ☐ **Spouse** was 65 or older ☐ Blind } **Enter number of boxes checked** ▶ 20a ☐

b If you are married filing separately and your spouse itemizes deductions, see page 30 and check here . . . . . . ▶ 20b ☐

21 Enter the **standard deduction** for your filing status. **But** see page 31 if you checked any box on line 20a or 20b **OR** if someone can claim you as a dependent.
- Single—$4,250
- Married filing jointly or Qualifying widow(er)—$7,100
- Head of household—$6,250
- Married filing separately—$3,550

21

22 Subtract line 21 from line 19. If line 21 is more than line 19, enter -0-. 22

23 Multiply $2,700 by the total number of exemptions claimed on line 6d. 23

24 Subtract line 23 from line 22. If line 23 is more than line 22, enter -0-. This is your **taxable income.** ▶ 24

Tax, credits, and payments

25 Find the tax on the amount on line 24 (see page 31). 25

26 Credit for child and dependent care expenses. Attach Schedule 2. 26

27 Credit for the elderly or the disabled. Attach Schedule 3. 27

28 Child tax credit (see page 32). 28

29 Education credits. Attach Form 8863. 29

30 Adoption credit. Attach Form 8839. 30

31 Add lines 26 through 30. These are your **total credits.** 31

32 Subtract line 31 from line 25. If line 31 is more than line 25, enter -0-. 32

33 Advance earned income credit payments from Form(s) W-2. 33

34 Add lines 32 and 33. This is your **total tax.** ▶ 34

35 Total Federal income tax withheld from Forms W-2 and 1099. 35

36 1998 estimated tax payments and amount applied from 1997 return. 36

37a **Earned income credit.** Attach Schedule EIC if you have a qualifying child. 37a

b Nontaxable earned income: amount ▶ and type ▶

38 Additional child tax credit. Attach Form 8812. 38

39 Add lines 35, 36, 37a, and 38. These are your **total payments.** ▶ 39

Refund

Have it directly deposited! See page 43 and fill in 41b, 41c, and 41d.

40 If line 39 is more than line 34, subtract line 34 from line 39. This is the amount you **overpaid.** 40

41a Amount of line 40 you want **refunded to you.** 41a

b Routing number ☐☐☐☐☐☐☐☐☐ c Type: ☐ Checking ☐ Savings

d Account number ☐☐☐☐☐☐☐☐☐☐☐☐☐☐☐☐☐

42 Amount of line 40 you want **applied to your 1999 estimated tax.** 42

Amount you owe

43 If line 34 is more than line 39, subtract line 39 from line 34. This is the **amount you owe.** For details on how to pay, see page 44. 43

44 Estimated tax penalty (see page 44). 44

Sign here

Joint return? See page 19. Keep a copy for your records.

Under penalties of perjury, I declare that I have examined this return and accompanying schedules and statements, and to the best of my knowledge and belief, they are true, correct, and accurately list all amounts and sources of income I received during the tax year. Declaration of preparer (other than the taxpayer) is based on all information of which the preparer has any knowledge.

Your signature	Date	Your occupation	Daytime telephone number (optional)
Spouse's signature. If joint return, BOTH must sign.	Date	Spouse's occupation	( )

Paid preparer's use only

Preparer's signature	Date	Check if self-employed ☐	Preparer's social security no.
Firm's name (or yours if self-employed) and address			EIN
			ZIP code

1040A—CHILD TAX CREDIT WORKSHEET

Child Tax Credit Worksheet–Line 28

▶ Keep for your records.

Do Not File

1. $400.00 ______ . Multiply and enter the result . . . . 1. ______
Enter number of qualifying children (see page 32)

2. Enter the amount from Form 1040A, line 19 . . . . . 2. ______

3. Is line 2 above more than $55,000?

☐ **No.** Skip lines 3 through 5, enter -0- on line 6, and go to line 7.

☐ **Yes.** Enter: $75,000 if single, head of household, or qualifying widow(er); $110,000 if married filing jointly; $55,000 if married filing separately . . . . . 3. ______

4. Subtract line 3 from line 2. If zero or less, enter -0- here and on line 6, and go to line 7 . . . . 4. ______

5. Divide line 4 by $1,000. If the result is not a whole number, round it up to the next higher whole number (for example, round 0.01 to 1) . . . . 5. ______

6. Multiply $50 by the number on line 5 . . . . 6. ______

7. Subtract line 6 from line 1. If zero or less, **stop here;** you **cannot** take this credit . 7. ______

8. Enter the amount from Form 1040A, line 25 . . . . . 8. ______

9. Is line 1 above more than $800?

☐ **No.** Add the amounts from Form 1040A, lines 26, 27, and 29. Enter the total.

☐ **Yes.** Enter the amount from the worksheet on page 34. } 9. ______

10. Subtract line 9 above from line 8 . . . . 10. ______

11. **Child tax credit.** Enter the **smaller** of line 7 or line 10 here and on Form 1040A, line 28 ▶ 11. ______

TIP *If line 1 above is more than $800, you may be able to take the* ***Additional Child Tax Credit.*** *See page 32.*

EIC—PAGE 1

SCHEDULE EIC (Form 1040A or 1040) Department of the Treasury Internal Revenue Service (99)	**Earned Income Credit (Qualifying Child Information)** ► Attach to Form 1040A or 1040. ► See instructions on back.	OMB No. 1545-0074 **1998** Attachment Sequence No. **43**
Name(s) shown on return		**Your social security number**

Before you begin . . .

- See the instructions for Form 1040A, lines 37a and 37b, or Form 1040, lines 59a and 59b, to find out if you can take this credit.
- If you can take the credit, fill in the Earned Income Credit Worksheet in the Form 1040A or Form 1040 instructions to figure your credit. **But if you want the IRS to figure it for you, see instructions on back.**

Then, you **must** complete and attach Schedule EIC only if you have a qualifying child (see boxes on back).

Information About Your Qualifying Child or Children

If you have more than two qualifying children, you only have to list two to get the maximum credit.

Caution: *If you do not attach Schedule EIC and fill in all the lines that apply, it will take us longer to process your return and issue your refund.*	**Child 1**		**Child 2**	
	First name	Last name	First name	Last name
1 Child's name				
2 Child's year of birth	19__ __		19__ __	
3 If the child was born **before 1980** AND—				
a was **under age 24** at the end of 1998 **and** a student, check "Yes," **OR**	☐ Yes		☐ Yes	
b was permanently and totally disabled (see back), check "Yes"	☐ Yes		☐ Yes	
4 Enter the child's social security number .				
5 Child's relationship to you (for example, son, grandchild, etc.)				
6 Number of months child lived with you in the United States in 1998	months		months	

TIP: Do you want the earned income credit added to your take-home pay in 1999? To see if you qualify, get **Form W-5** from your employer or by calling the IRS at 1-800-TAX-FORM (1-800-829-3676).

For Paperwork Reduction Act Notice, see Form 1040A or 1040 instructions. Cat. No. 13339M **Schedule EIC (Form 1040A or 1040) 1998**

EIC—PAGE 2

Schedule EIC (Form 1040A or 1040) 1998 Page **2**

Instructions

Purpose of Schedule

If you can take the earned income credit and have a qualifying child, use Schedule EIC to give information about that child. To figure the amount of your credit, use the worksheet in the instructions for Form 1040A, lines 37a and 37b, or Form 1040, lines 59a and 59b.

If you want the IRS to figure the credit for you, enter "EIC" directly to the right of line 37a of Form 1040A or line 59a of Form 1040. Also, enter the amount and type of any nontaxable earned income in the spaces provided on Form 1040A, line 37b, or Form 1040, line 59b, and attach Schedule EIC to your return.

Line 1

Enter each qualifying child's name.

Line 3a

If your child was born **before 1980** but was under age 24 at the end of 1998 and a student, check "Yes."

Your child was a **student** if, during any 5 months of 1998, he or she—

- Was enrolled as a full-time student at a school, or
- Took a full-time, on-farm training course. The course had to be given by a school or a state, county, or local government agency.

A **school** includes technical, trade, and mechanical schools. It does not include on-the-job training courses, correspondence schools, or night schools.

Line 3b

If your child was born **before 1980** and was permanently and totally disabled during any part of 1998, check "Yes."

A person is **permanently and totally disabled** if **both** of the following apply.

1. He or she cannot engage in any substantial gainful activity because of a physical or mental condition.

2. A doctor determines the condition has lasted or can be expected to last continuously for at least a year or can lead to death.

Line 4

You must enter your child's social security number (SSN) on line 4 unless he or she was born and died in 1998. If you do not enter the correct SSN, at the time we process your return, we may reduce or disallow your credit. If your child was born and died in 1998 and did not have an SSN, enter "Died" on line 4 **and** attach a copy of the child's birth certificate.

If your child does not have an SSN, apply for one by filing **Form SS-5** with your local Social Security Administration office. It usually takes about 2 weeks to get a number. If your child will not have an SSN by April 15, 1999, you can get an automatic 4-month extension by filing **Form 4868** with the IRS by that date.

Line 6

Enter the number of months your child lived with you in your home in the United States during 1998. (If you were in the military on extended active duty outside the United States, your home is considered to be in the United States during that duty period.) Do not enter more than 12. Count temporary absences, such as for school, vacation, or medical care, as time lived in your home. If the child lived with you for more than half of 1998 but less than 7 months, enter "7" on line 6.

Exception. If your child, including a foster child, was born or died in 1998 and your home was the child's home for the entire time he or she was alive during 1998, enter "12" on line 6.

Qualifying Child

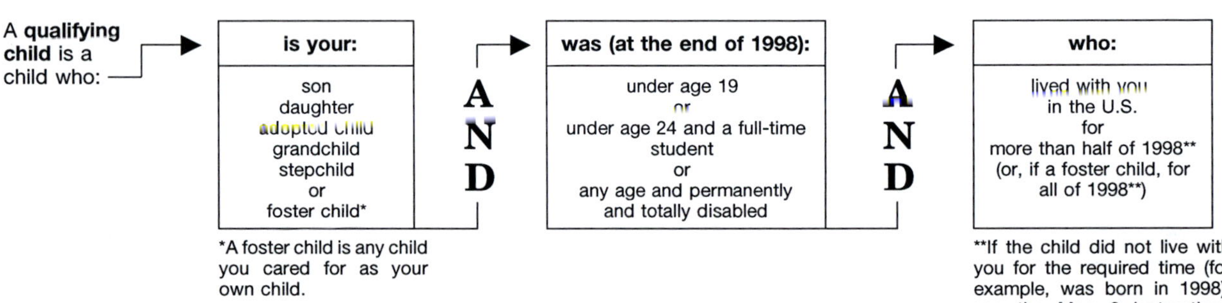

If the child was married or is also a qualifying child of another person (other than your spouse if filing a joint return), special rules apply. For details, see the instructions for Form 1040A, lines 37a and 37b, or Form 1040, lines 59a and 59b. Also, the child must have an SSN (as defined in those instructions) unless he or she was born and died in 1998.

Glossary

Accountant—Person who prepares financial reports and gives financial advice. Many accountants prepare tax returns. An accountant with a special license from the state is called a CPA (certified public accountant).

Assistor—Person who works for the IRS to help individuals with questions about their income tax forms.

Attorney—Lawyer. Some lawyers specialize in tax law.

Audit—A check of your tax return by the IRS. The IRS is looking for mistakes.

Claim—To list. For example, you list, or claim, deductions and exemptions on your income tax forms.

Deadline—Last date by which tax returns should be completed and mailed to the IRS.

Dependent—Person who is financially supported by someone else; usually a child. A person is considered by the IRS to be your dependent if five conditions are met. (See the section in Chapter 4, "Who is a dependent?")

Dividends—Money you receive from stocks or investments. Dividends are a type of taxable income.

Earned income credit—A special credit for low income parents who earned less than a certain amount. More than $3,000 may be received for this credit. However, certain conditions must be met. (See "Schedule EIC" in the Appendix.)

Earnings—Money you receive, usually from your employer.

Employer—The person or company that hires you to work.

Exemption—Amount of money you may subtract from your income for each dependent. You are also allowed an exemption for yourself if you support yourself. Your spouse is also allowed an exemption.

Federal—Related to the government in Washington, D.C. Federal taxes are collected by the United States government. This tax money is then distributed throughout the country to pay for many different federal programs.

Fee—Charge or payment. Tax preparers who fill out your income tax forms usually charge you a fee for this service.

Filing status—How you define your family situation for tax purposes. You must select one of five choices: single, head of household, widow/widower with dependent child, married couple filing their income tax return together (jointly), married couple filing their income tax returns separately.

Gross pay—Total amount of pay you earn before your employer withholds federal and state taxes.

Head of household—Special filing status for single person who supports certain relatives. This filing status is often used by a single person with children. (See the section in Chapter 4, "What is your filing status?")

Income—Money you receive, such as salary, tips, interest from the bank, and lottery winnings. These are only a few examples of income; there are many more types, such as alimony and money received from rentals.

Interest—Money a bank pays you for savings you have deposited there. You must report all of the interest you receive on your tax return forms. (You pay interest to the bank if you have a loan.)

IRA—Individual retirement account. An IRA is a special savings account for workers, similar to a pension or retirement plan at work. You can deduct IRA contributions, up to a certain limit, from your income. IRAs represent another way to reduce the amount of taxes that you must pay to the government.

IRS—The Internal Revenue Service—the federal agency responsible for collecting tax moneys owed to the federal government.

ITIN—The Individual Taxpayer Identification number can be substituted for the Social Security number for tax purposes when taxpayers and their dependents are not eligible for a Social Security number. Use Form W-7 to apply for an ITI number.

Itemized deduction—The actual amount of expenditures you may subtract from your income. Use this amount only if it is larger than the standard deduction.

Net pay—Amount of pay you receive after your employer withholds federal and state taxes.

Penalty—A fine for not following IRS rules. Usually, the IRS charges you extra money if you send in your income tax forms late or if you do not pay all of the tax money that you owe. In very serious cases, such as fraud, penalties may include going to jail.

Sighted—Not blind. Only sighted people should complete the 1040EZ. Blind people should complete the 1040A form because an extra exemption is allowed by the government to blind taxpayers. This exemption is only listed on the 1040A and the 1040 forms, not on the 1040EZ.

Standard deduction—A fixed amount of money that the government allows you to subtract from the income you report to the IRS. The amount varies according to your filing status.

State—Related to the government of the individual 50 U.S. states—for example, Oregon and Arkansas. State taxes are collected by the states. This tax money is then distributed throughout the state to pay for many different state programs.

Support—Paying for such things as rent, food, clothes, medical and educational expenses for another person. Parents usually support their children.

Tax—Money collected by the state of the federal government to pay for programs they support.

Taxable income—Income upon which you must pay taxes. Not all income is taxed. Welfare benefits, workers' compensation benefits, and health insurance benefits are example of income that is not taxable. However, wages, tips, interest from the bank, and lottery winnings are examples of income that is taxed.

Tax-exempt—Not taxable. Some types of interest and dividends are not considered taxable because they are received from municipal bonds or from special tax-exempt agencies such as public utilities.

Tax return—Report you file every year to calculate your exact tax bill. Examples of tax return forms are the 1040EZ and 1040A.

W-2 form—The form your employer sends to you in January of each year that indicates how much you earned the year before and how much was deducted from your earnings to pay federal and state taxes.

W-4 form—Form completed by the employee that tells the employer the amount of money that should be deducted from the gross pay and sent to the federal and state governments as taxes.

Wages—Money you are paid by your employer; salary.

Widow/widower—Person whose spouse has died. *Widow* refers to a woman; *widower* refers to a man. For tax purposes, it is a special filing status for individuals who lost their spouse less than two years ago AND have not remarried AND who have at least one dependent child.

Withhold—To deduct money from your pay. Your employer withholds money from your paycheck to pay federal and state taxes. The amount your employer withholds is only an estimate of what you owe. The yearly tax return form is used to calculate your exact tax bill.